One Man's Journey

The Untold Story of the

Quest for Truth

Donald T. Hardison, II

ISBN: 979-8989561902 (eBook)
ISBN: 979-8989561919 (Paperback)
ISBN: 979-8989561926 (Hardcover)

Edited with care by Elizabeth's Writing Corner
https://www.elizabethswritingcorner.com.

To every one who suffers loss and endures trials, tribulations, and tragedy—both great and small.

To all those who feel alone and misunderstood, thinking that there is nobody who truly cares.

Table of Contents

Introduction

Have you ever thought about taking a journey? Perhaps you are already on your own journey right now. Does the thought of starting out anew or continuing on your current path terrify you?

You may have thoughts like, "What if I get lost?" "What will happen to me as I travel this unknown path?"

Or perhaps you have spoken with others and shared your ideas with them, only to be laughed at or called crazy. Do you feel like no matter how hard you try to explain what you're going through you're only going to be further misunderstood and ridiculed?

All the while, this mysterious longing continues to echo inside of you. Adventure is just begging for you to come and see what life can look like outside of the realm of your everyday norm.

I invite you to travel with me as we walk side by side on my own adventure. This journey begins in a holler and leads us onto a path that winds beside the still waters. It continues into the valleys below and climbs up to the high peaks of the mountains. The road is dark at times, and the destination often appears to be impossible to reach.

There is a journey like this for each one of us, just waiting to be explored. If you are willing to simply step out on this wild adventure, it will even change your life. I just dare you to believe!

This is my story.

Chapter 1

Home Is Where the Heart Is

was born in the spring of 1976 to a loving couple in their twenties. My father worked for Jeep and my mother was a housewife. They had an amazing love for one another that I've never seen before and have yet to see again to this day. Their love was unique and truly their own.

My parents married at a very young age—my dad was eighteen and my mom was fifteen. Since they were born and raised in Ohio, they weren't legally able to get married until they were both eighteen, but they didn't let that stop them. They were madly in love and knew they were meant to be together, no matter what.

So, my dad and my mom hatched a plan to get married in Asheville, North Carolina, since it was legal in that state to marry at a young age with the consent of my mom's parents. They all packed up— my father, my mother, my mother's sister and her husband, and my grandmother—and drove the eight-hour trip to Asheville.

My parents were married by the Justice of the Peace on June 26. However, my grandmother would not allow them to consummate the marriage until they were married in the Catholic church! This meant that they would be sleeping in two separate hotel rooms for the night, even though they had already been married in the eyes of the state. It was settled—my mother, my aunt, and my grandmother stayed in one room, and my dad and my uncle were in another.

The next morning, they all jumped back into the car and headed back home to Ohio. That very same day, on June 27, my parents were married for a second time in a simple ceremony at the local Catholic church.

My parents had four children—two boys and two girls. We all grew up in a very loving home. My mother, being the Suzie Homemaker that she was, loved to cook hot meals for us every day. She'd set the table, bring out the amazing dishes she worked hard to prepare, and invite us all to sit down as a family for dinner. As we ate the delicious food, we talked with one another and shared how our day had gone.

Did I mention that my mom also loved to bake? She took great joy in taking care of her family from making homemade meals to baking desserts, from keeping a clean house to interior decorating.

My mom had a passion for reading, writing, and the arts. She loved the work of master painters like Leonardo da Vinci, Monet, and Picasso. She was also highly involved with redevelopment efforts and community activities within the neighborhood we grew up in. My mom was even responsible for naming a local organization that was founded to help people who needed assistance.

My mother did it all! She was meticulous—a perfectionist, some would say—and took care of every detail, all while raising four children who were close in age.

Of course, my father put in his fair share of effort by helping when he got home from work. Whatever my mom couldn't get to, my dad completed. They were an amazing team, enjoying every opportunity to take us on exciting outings— local parks, picnics, camping, the zoo, art museums, theater plays, and family vacations.

My parents dropped out of high school in the ninth grade, which wasn't an uncommon thing to do back then. As long as you could add, subtract, multiply, divide, spell, read, and write, you were able to get a job in those days. Years later, my mother went on to get her GED.

My father preferred to learn from life itself, otherwise known as the School of Hard Knocks. He couldn't read very well and didn't feel that his schooling would benefit him in the future. After all, my dad was a hardworking young man, had already landed himself a job that paid good money, and had no need for a high school diploma. My mother eventually taught him how to read, since they enjoyed reading books together.

My parents took great pleasure in raising us. Each one of us was different and unique in our own ways and were treated as individuals with our own distinct personalities.

We always enjoyed a lot of bonding time as a family. My dad loved to take us boys fishing, and my mom enjoyed taking the girls out. Then my parents would switch, making sure we had ample time with each one of them. Of course, we also went out as a whole family.

We prayed together every day. As my mother always said, "A family who prays together, stays together." I'd say we were a pretty close-knit family, and it made my parents proud.

My father taught me all the outdoor tasks he regularly took care of—cutting the grass, landscaping, shoveling snow, raking leaves, and cutting, splitting, and stacking wood. He also was efficient in automotive repair and carpentry work, a true jack of all trades.

My mother taught me many different things as well, including how to keep a clean house and how to do the laundry. I had a lot of chores growing up.

As my mom liked to say, "A clean home is a happy home." She always had a way with words, giving a simple catch phrase for every situation to bring us a deeper understanding about life.

My parents spent a lot of time teaching me responsibilities and explaining how hard work paid off at the end of every day. They knew that the lessons I learned when I was young would develop a strong character in me that would last a lifetime.

When I was eleven years old, I started working for the widows in my neighborhood. They were up there in age and could always use the help. I'd spend time cutting grass, raking leaves, pruning rose bushes, pulling weeds, and edging sidewalks. I totally enjoyed it, even if I got pricked by thorns a few times or suffered a few minor calluses here and there.

The widows I worked for also enjoyed my company, plus they always made me a nice lunch with iced tea or hot chocolate, depending on the season. After the job was done for the day, we'd sit and talk. They asked me how I was doing and what I wanted to become one day. They spoke about my work ethic and how happy they were to have me.

Each lady shared her story with me about her beloved husband who passed away in the Vietnam war, showing me the pictures of that brave man that she kept around the house. The widows even talked about their children, if they had any, and how they had become too busy with their own lives to come visit and spend time with them. They were strong women who had been through it all.

In many ways, I felt like I had become a son to each of them. They watched me grow from a young boy into a teenager, always complimenting me on how handsome I was turning out to be and how any girl would be lucky to have me one day. To be honest, I was quite fond of these older ladies as well. They taught me a lot about love and life and the many hardships that life would bring.

Plus, I was doing the Lord's work by visiting and working for these women who were lonely and had no one to care for them anymore. After all, caring for others is what they knew best. As they always practiced, "A cookie here, and a cookie there, and one for the walk home."

There was one widow in particular who I was very close to named Ms. Garvin. She lost her husband in the war, never had any children, never remarried, and lived alone. My parents actually rented our townhouse from Ms. Garvin, so we lived next door to her as I grew up. She eventually willed our house to my parents.

I saw Ms. Garvin every morning as she peeked out her windows or swept both of her front and back porches. I always waved to her or said, "Good morning!" whenever I saw her, but she didn't seem very friendly.

She'd give a quick wave and say, "Now be on your way," as she swept the mat in front of her door. If she was inside and keeping an eye on the neighborhood, she'd quickly replace the curtain and act as if she didn't see me waving to her.

I always felt sad for Ms. Garvin. At times, I was even a little scared of her! It was as if she didn't want to be bothered, but I continued to ask her if she needed my help with anything, even when I always received the same response from her to be on my way.

From my point of view, Ms. Garvin was old, and giving her a helping hand was the right thing to do. Of course, she was tough and had done everything by herself for her entire life. She was set in her ways, especially when it came to cutting her grass. She was very serious about keeping her yard well-maintained and took great pride in it.

Every Saturday morning, I would look out the window to see Ms. Garvin hard at work. She got up bright and early, getting straight to it—cutting the grass, pulling weeds, and tending to her prize-winning rose garden. You see, there was this unspoken competition going on between the women in the neighborhood—not only whose roses were better, but whose were the best!

One Saturday morning, I looked outside and noticed that Ms. Garvin's grass hadn't been cut. I went downstairs and found my dad.

"Is Ms. Garvin all right?" I asked him.

Dad looked at me curiously and wondered, "Why do you ask?"

I told him, "I noticed that Ms. Garvin hasn't cut her grass yet."

So, he went next door to check on our landlady. When Dad came back, he told me that Ms. Garvin wasn't feeling well and had a cold.

At that point, I asked my dad, "Would be all right if I cut the grass for her?" I figured it would make her happy.

Dad said with a smile, "Sure, why not? I think she'd like that!"

So, I went straight outside and began to cut Ms. Garvin's grass. As I busily worked, I noticed her peeking out the window at me every now and then, trying to keep an eye on my work without me noticing!

As soon as I finished the grass, I started to pull the weeds along her sidewalk and the stairs leading up to the house. I knew for a fact that if there was one thing she couldn't stand, it was weeds sprouting up all over the place!

After I finished the weeding, I headed straight for her flower garden. Now, I knew that NO ONE set foot among Ms. Garvin's roses except for her, but she was sick today. After all, weeds don't stop growing and popping up in places where they're not wanted just because somebody gets sick.

I had just knelt down beside a towering rose bush and yanked two big fistfuls of weeds from the ground when, all of a sudden, there she was!

"What are you doing?" Ms. Garvin asked me. Before I had a chance to give her an adequate explanation, she was asking to see my hands.

I stood back up and sheepishly held up my hands for inspection. They were filled with dirt and the remnants of what I thought were weeds.

Ms. Garvin then took the collection of my attempts at weeding and pulled out two different kinds of leaves.

"Do you know what plants these two leaves belong to?" she asked me.

Of course, I had no clue, so she began to show me the differences between a weed and a newly sprouted rose bush. I had pulled both!

To my surprise, Ms. Garvin wasn't mad at me, and she didn't yell at me when I quickly apologized for my mistake.

Instead, she just looked at me and said, "That's okay. You didn't know any better, but you do now. Go ahead and continue, but make sure to be careful with what you're pulling."

She also gave me another bit of information that I didn't know about—she liked the dirt patted back in place in every area where weeds had been pulled. After each invading plant was removed, roots and all, there were not to be any ruts left in her prize-winning garden. Everything was pristine!

From that day, Ms. Garvin and I became extremely close. Come to find out, she had all kinds of work that needed to be done, both inside the house and out in the yard.

So, every day after school, I made it a point to go over there to tackle her laundry list of tasks that was stuck to her refrigerator by one of her many magnets. Each time I completed a chore, I enjoyed checking it off the list.

It seemed like, no matter how much I accomplished, new things were always being added to the list. I didn't mind, as I kept eyeing how much each chore paid and the grand total at the bottom of the sheet. As I found out, Ms. Garvin was adding tasks to the list because she had become attached to me and wanted to make sure I'd always come back to spend time with her.

Every afternoon, I'd head over to find Ms. Garvin sitting at her kitchen table with her apron on, waiting for me with a warm welcome. I made sure to ask her what she wanted done first. She gave me a quick hug and a kiss on my cheek, and then I was ready to get started.

When I first started working for Ms. Garvin, she explained to me that she would pay me every Friday. There was just one catch—for every ten dollars I made, I would only get eight. The other two dollars would go into an envelope and be given to her church to help feed the homeless, poor, and needy. That sounded right to me, so we shook hands. You see, that's what two people did back in the day after negotiating and agreeing upon a deal.

As time passed, my parents talked about how they were able to see a definite change in Ms. Garvin. She baked cookies and homemade bread, bringing the gifts to us fresh out of the oven, always using the excuse that she had made too much and didn't want anything to go to waste.

She'd even come out of the house and sit on her front porch, just waiting for the opportunity to talk to my mom and dad. I remember her picking me up, setting me on her lap, and all of us drinking her homemade lemonade as Ms. Garvin and my parents chatted back and forth.

As a matter of fact, Ms. Garvin became so attached to me that if I didn't show up at her house after I got home from school by a certain time, she'd come knocking.

"Where's my little Donnie at?" she asked my parents, looking forward to spending time with me.

All the while, I felt the same way. Ms. Garvin was a delight to be around, being full of joy and compassion.

Some nights, she'd make me dinner and serve it with a cold glass of milk to drink. I remember her telling me that milk was good for me because it would give me strong bones, as that was something I would need as I would soon grow up to be a man.

After supper, we washed the dishes together. Ms. Garvin would wash, and I stood next to her, drying the dishes off with a rag and placing them all neatly in the right order in her cupboard.

When the kitchen was cleaned, we were off to the living room to sit on the couch together and watch the Billy Graham crusades. Ms. Garvin loved watching Billy Graham and told me everything she knew about him. His deep southern voice and style of preaching was always easy on the ears and a pleasure to watch.

Billy's story always inspired me, and in many ways, I wanted to be just like him, having the freedom to travel around and help people in need.

My parents witnessed a significant change in Ms. Garvin, just as if she was coming back to life again after many years. Her transformation was prompted by her desire to have someone to love and care for. Her love for me and my love for her did just that. I was just what she needed, and she was just what I needed.

My parents' hearts were truly touched as they saw all these things take place, but they weren't the only ones who noticed what was happening. Others in the neighborhood recognized and welcomed the change in Ms. Garvin as well.

A few years later, I was getting ready for bed and heard a loud thump that sounded like something heavy had fallen and hit the ground. I knew that the noise didn't come from our side of the house, so I ran to wake up my dad and tell him what I heard. I asked him to go and check on Ms. Garvin.

My dad jumped out of bed and went next door while I sat with my mom. He stayed over at Ms. Garvin's for what seemed like forever.

When my dad came back, he called my mother and me downstairs and asked me to go into the living room and wait for them there. He had to tell my mom privately what happened.

As they walked into the living room, I remember that my dad put me on his lap and my mom sat close beside both of us. I asked my dad if Ms. Garvin was all right.

He replied, "Ms. Garvin passed away and went to be with the Lord."

I felt relieved and said, "That's okay, she'll come back and see me!" You see, I was only eight at the time and had never experienced death before.

After three days, I still hadn't seen her, so I asked my parents, "When is Ms. Garvin coming back to see me? I miss her."

My parents took me upstairs and got me dressed in some nice clothes, telling me that they were taking me to see her and that she was just down the street.

As we headed out the door and approached the building where I would see Ms. Garvin, I began to feel scared. I knew that building was a place where people went in, but they never came out! You see, my friends and I attended a Catholic school and always talked about that building during recess since it was right across the street from us. We knew it was a funeral home, and that dead people were in there!

At that point, I knew something was very wrong. If Ms. Garvin was in that place, I would go in to see her once, but then I would never see her again.

As we walked in, I saw people standing around her casket, looking down at her but not talking to her. I let go of my dad's hand and ran straight for her. Leaping over the kneeler, I jumped into the casket and tried to put my arms around Ms. Garvin to give her a hug.

She was cold and stiff. I could no longer feel the warmth of her touch or see the sparkle in her eyes that she always gave me when I spent time with her.

I began to cry, begging her not to leave me. "Please don't go, Ms. Garvin," I said, "I love you!"

It was too late. Her spirit had already left her body.

All the people in the room saw what was happening and immediately began to cry along with me, saying, "Bless his little heart!" Everyone had heard stories of how Ms. Garvin had changed over the years and how I played a huge part in that.

My father was shocked since my sudden actions and emotions came out of nowhere. Yet, he completely understood, as did everyone else. He gently picked me up out of the casket and held me tightly in his arms.

I remember him telling me, "I know this hurts, Son, but she's in a better place."

I have never forgotten about Ms. Garvin and, to this day, still carry fond memories of the good times we once shared.

Chapter 2

A Man of Integrity

My mother seemed to raise me quite differently from my brother and sisters. She was strict and stern with me, telling me that she was raising a man, and a man of integrity at that.

I remember how my mom would challenge me in my studies, teaching me how to go the extra mile to look into certain things. As I began to research this and that, we would have lots of discussions about all kinds of subjects. If my mom wasn't pleased with what I brought to the table, she would immediately encourage me to look further into the matter.

In response to my mom's challenge, I often found myself going to the library and spending countless hours scouring many different books. I spent so much time there that I came to know all the librarians personally.

The librarians were always very helpful, wondering what I was researching on that particular day and asking me if I needed assistance finding anything. They even taught me how to use the Library of Congress Classification System just in case they were busy helping someone else when I needed to locate a particular resource.

Between school, homework, household chores, working for the neighbors, and spending time with family, I stayed pretty busy as a child.

I remember one summer afternoon, coming home after a long hard day of work. It was a Friday, so it was payday. In my pocket, I had all the money I made during the week in my various jobs helping the neighborhood widows.

I was very excited, to say the least, since I had cleared $200 in just that week. At the time, that was a lot of money for an eleven-year-old kid! I felt proud of myself. My hard work was paying off and I was making great memories while learning the tricks of the trade.

I remember sliding into a chair at the kitchen table after pulling the neatly folded bills from my pocket. I began to carefully recount the cash, making sure I hadn't lost anything on my way home.

Just then, my mother walked into the kitchen and eyeballed me. She asked, "Whatcha got there?"

I was excited to tell her about my earnings.

She asked me, "What are you planning to do with all that money?"

I told her that since I was continuing to work and picking up new customers along the way, I was just planning on saving my earnings somewhere safe in my room.

My mom, however, had other plans for my hard-earned cash, starting with some hard life lessons that I would shortly become acquainted with. She sat down across from me and proceeded to talk to me about expenses—rent, groceries, electric and gas bills, clothing, my schooling, my bedroom furniture, TV and cable, the cost of gas to run the lawnmower—making me aware that nothing in life comes for free.

"You have to spend money to make money," she quipped. "The world meets nobody halfway."

She told me it was time I started to pay rent. When I quickly looked up at her, I could see that she wasn't at all joking with me. She was dead serious.

My mother disappeared for a few moments and came back with a stack of papers, showing me all the bills and receipts that she regularly took care of. I began to see how much it cost to run a household on a monthly basis. As she pointed out everything in the greatest of detail, my mother explained how I would one day be a man of my own and would have to take care of all of this by myself.

"This seems like an awful lot of money," I said in surprise.

"Which is why you need to learn how to share in the load and pay your part," my mom replied. "And there's no time like the present to begin."

So, she began. A little here for rent, a little there for groceries, and let's not forget schooling and furniture! After divvying up what I initially thought was all mine, I was left with forty dollars. Another thirty of that remainder was going to be used to set up a savings account, leaving me with just ten dollars—five dollars used for gas money to get my mom to the bank and back, and the other five dollars for me.

What started out to be an exciting day for me suddenly went from good to bad! I looked up at my mom in disbelief.

"But my brother and sisters don't work," I said, "and they sure don't have to pay rent! Why me?"

My mother looked at me straight in the face. "I am raising a man," she replied firmly. "And not just any man—a man of integrity!"

This was something that my mother reminded me of quite frequently, and it did nothing to relieve the crushing disappointment I was feeling.

I did the only thing I knew I could do—I went to talk to my dad. When I told him everything that happened, he thought at first that my mom was just playing with me. He told me that he would talk to her and straighten everything out.

Later, after my dad's talk with my mom, her decision was final. Even he couldn't change her mind! Although he didn't agree with her point of view, he wasn't going to interfere and left it up to my mother and me to work it out. So, I continued to help pay for the household expenses for as long as I lived in my parents' home.

I remember another time when I needed some new clothes. In fact, I desperately needed a pair of work shoes and some sturdy jeans because the clothes I wore after school were raggedy, to say the least. The patches in my knees from previous holes were no longer holding up. The soles in my shoes were separated at the toes and heels to the point that they flapped when I walked. I even used duct tape to hold everything together!

The neighborhood kids pointed and laughed at me whenever they passed by while I was working or when they saw me walking home. I could hear them whispering to each other and making fun of me.

I had enough! After all, I wasn't poor. I was a hardworking man and had my own money. I deserved to have the respect of a working man as well.

So, I went to my mom and asked her to take me to the store. I planned to get what I so desperately needed, and I even offered to give her gas money and take her to lunch as well. I figured it was the responsible thing to do and hoped that she would see the respect I had learned from the lessons she was instilling into my mind and heart. Plus, I figured she couldn't say no when lunch was on me.

My mother looked me up and down, and then she asked me, "How do you plan to buy these things, hmm?"

I immediately responded, "Well, I have a savings account, don't I?"

"Yes, you do," my mother admitted, but then was quick to add, "But as you said yourself, it's a savings account, so it cannot be touched. After all, that's what a savings account is for—savings!"

Not about to be deterred, I replied, "Hold on! I'll be right back."

I ran upstairs to my bedroom and grabbed the little bit of money I had stashed away in a shoebox. Seeing how I only received a small stipend for my weekly earnings, I always tucked it secretly away in my closet and had been doing so for quite some time.

I counted it quickly before heading back downstairs. I had $102, and while there were some bills, most of it was change. I returned to my mom in the kitchen.

"I have the money to buy what I need," I told her, beginning to explain my plan to her in great detail. I could tell that my mom was listening carefully as I added the gas money, the lunch money, and the clothing money out loud for her.

"But what about the sales tax?" she inquired, telling me to go get a calculator and run the numbers through again to be sure.

I did as she directed and determined that, after all expenses were paid, I would still have a few dollars left over. So, I asked my mom once more if she would take me.

Unfortunately, my mom simply said, "No."

I replied, "Okay, Mom, thanks anyway. Can I at least ask Dad to take me when he gets home?"

"Sure, you can ask him," she responded, "but he's going to be very tired when he gets here. He'll want to relax after a hard day's work."

"Okay, I'll keep that in mind," I said. "It won't hurt to ask," and that was that.

So, I was back to waiting for my dad to get home, which was usually around 3:15 PM. I knew that time by heart because I used to stand at the window every afternoon when I was a little boy, staring out into the street and waiting for his truck to pull up in the driveway. I was always excited to see him, and it was the highlight of my day!

These days, I was much older, and I rarely had time to stand around. Today, however, I had a definite need, so I would have to make an exception.

As soon as my dad pulled in, I ran out to his truck, meeting him in the driveway just as he was grabbing his lunchbox out of the passenger seat. We were always excited to see each other, so it was only after a hug and kiss on the cheek that I brought up the conversation I had with my mom.

"If you have time, can you take me to the store?" I asked hopefully. I offered him the same thing I had initially mentioned to my mom—gas money and lunch on me.

My dad replied, "Let me see your mom, talk to her, and see what's going on first. We'll take it from there."

"Okay, thank you, Dad," I said, doing my best to wait patiently for him to give me an answer. As my dad headed inside, I couldn't help but overhear him talking to my mom, asking her why she didn't take me to the store.

She replied, "I didn't think he had enough to cover the taxes for his purchases."

So, my dad told her that he was going to run me out to the store and that we'd be back in a little bit. He gave my mom a kiss, and we headed out.

As we jumped into his truck, my dad turned to me and asked, "Now what about this lunch? You know that your mother is making us dinner right now."

"Oh, come on, Dad," I said. "I won't tell if you don't!"

We decided that a little snack wouldn't hurt, so we headed toward my dad's favorite place, Coney Island. He loved the breakfasts that they served 24/7. Plus, they were cheap, and you couldn't beat their cooking!

On the way there, my dad asked me what store I wanted to go to.

"Kmart," I answered. It was close to the restaurant we were going to, which was an added bonus. Then, I asked my dad how much he wanted for gas. I planned to give him a little more than I had budgeted for my mom, knowing that his truck burned more fuel than my mother's van.

My dad looked from me to the money in my hand and then back again at my face, giving me a tiny smile in the process. I didn't see any tears in his eyes, but I heard a funny little catch in his throat as he told me to put the money away.

"I don't need your money, Son," my dad said, explaining to me that he wasn't my mother and didn't really understand why she was so hard on me. What he did know was that he definitely didn't need me to cover the gas. This was now guy time, and he had everything covered!

I remember thinking to myself, "What a lucky boy I am to have such a great dad!"

As we walked into Coney Island and the delicious smells from the kitchen hit us, I told my dad to get whatever he wanted off the menu.

"My treat," I told him proudly.

My dad once again gave me that funny little smile, appearing a bit confused as I continued to explain.

"Dad, this is what men of integrity do! I'm your son, and I can surely take you out to eat. After all, look at everything you do for me!"

My dad simply replied that everything he did for me was from the bottom of his heart. "A father takes great pride in being able to provide for his family," he said, but he graciously left it up to me if I wanted to cover the bill.

It was settled, and I happily covered the bill for our quick "snack" that both of us thoroughly enjoyed.

Once we arrived at Kmart, I decided to make the trip inside as short as possible, knowing that my dad had a long and tiring day at work. First, we went to the boy's shoe section. I found a suitable pair, giving them a quick slip on and off to make sure they fit and felt comfortable. Then we were off to the clothing aisle so I could grab two pairs of Wrangler jeans. Even better, the jeans were on sale!

As we got to the register, I began putting everything on the conveyor belt.

My dad looked at me and asked, "Mind if I get a Milky Way?"

I knew they were his favorite. "Of course," I said gladly. "Grab two!"

So, he did, and then my dad suddenly remembered something. "You know, I forgot to grab some WD-40. Mind running back and grabbing some for me? I'll hold the line."

Always eager to please, I was off and running straight for the automotive department. Unfortunately, when I got to the correct spot, the

WD-40 was sitting high on a shelf—far too high for me to reach.

I eyeballed the nice and neat row of cans for a few seconds, glancing up and down the aisle and then looking skeptically at the rickety-looking shelving. I didn't dare climb up to reach a can and didn't know what else to do, so I headed back to the cash register.

As I trotted back, I prepared to tell my dad that I couldn't reach it. To my surprise, however, my dad was no longer at the register, and neither were my purchases!

Looking all around, I finally spotted my dad quietly standing by the door with a bag—with all of my purchases inside. I quickly caught onto the situation, realizing that he had sent me on a wild goose chase so he could pay for my items!

As I walked up to him, I said, "You didn't really need the WD-40, did you?"

My dad smiled and replied, "No, Son. I have six cans at home in the garage."

We both had a good chuckle, and then I said, "Thank you, Dad, but please let me pay you back."

My dad didn't reply, simply motioning for me to follow him out toward the truck while reaching into the bag and pulling out the two Milky Ways. He handed one to me and began to peel back the wrapper on the other for himself.

"Come on, Dad," I told him, shoving the candy bar back at him. "You know I don't like sweets very much. I wanted you to have two. Save the other for your lunch tomorrow while you're at work."

Once again, everything was settled. My father wouldn't take my money, but how could he say no to another Milky Way?

As we drove back home, he made sure to let me know that he was doing this from his heart. He always wanted me to remember how much he loved me.

Later that night, my mother came to my room while I was taking the tags off my new clothes while neatly folding and putting the jeans away.

"How much did you spend?" she asked me, looking around for a receipt.

I replied, "Actually, Dad bought this for me, and I offered to pay him back, but he wouldn't take it. Do you want me to pay you for everything?"

Just as we were about to get squared away, my dad suddenly appeared as if out of nowhere. He looked from me to my mother and then his eyes settled on me.

"Put your money away, Son," he said in a firm but gentle tone. "We don't need or want your money. Just know that we love you."

As my parents left my room and headed to their own, my mother simply said what any good mother would say after a new purchase.

"Make sure you take good care of what you just got so it will last a long time."

"I will, Mom," I promised, thanking them profusely before we all settled down for the night.

As I continued to learn what it meant to be a man of integrity, I faced many additional lessons, like how to think for myself, what it meant to demonstrate strong leadership, how to give compassion to others, and the importance of having respect, honor, dignity, mercy, and grace. Most of all, I understood the necessity of doing all things as if I was doing them for the Lord.

Those were the majors. Everything else fell within the concept of having morals and values that I was expected to practice every day.

As I was growing up, we always seemed to have a revolving door on our house. All kinds of people were always dropping by. Whether it was for prayer, for biblical council, or just to say hi, there was always something going on at our house.

Neighbors stopped in, pastors came by, several evangelists were in and out, and plenty of church folks were regular guests. Even the local police who patrolled our neighborhood often stopped by to chat, grab coffee, and eat a snack, while always asking for prayer for safety.

Once people came, they stayed for hours. They didn't need to wait for an invitation for dinner, refreshments, coffee, or something cold to drink. It was just a given that everyone would be welcomed and that all needs would be readily filled.

We children were taught to always serve our guests. We stood nearby, waiting for the opportunity to politely ask if our guests wanted a refill, but making sure to do it in such a way that did not interrupt their conversation. After all, "Children were to be seen, and not heard."

The people who came into our house always marveled at how polite and well-mannered we were. It was a sure testament to the home we grew up in and how our parents raised us.

As I continued to grow up, many people who came over would always stop in front of me, pat my head, and say that I was a special boy.

"The Lord is going to use you in a mighty way," they would tell me.

At times, my mother or father even called me to come in and join their meetings because these people wanted to pray over me.

I didn't mind since I made it a point to read my Bible every day and I understood the importance of prayer. I may not have understood what the people meant when they called me "special" or said that "the Lord is going to use you mightily one day."

It made me feel good to hear that the Lord had a plan for my life. I loved Him, and the stories I read about the way He worked in people's lives always caught my attention.

I remember asking my mom and my dad what the people meant by what they said about me.

They both looked at me and replied, "God has a special calling on your life. One day, He's going to ask you to do something special for Him."

I said, "Hmm, okay, but how will I know when He wants me to do it?"

They glanced at each other, looked back at me, and smiled. "Don't worry about that. When the day comes, He will make it very clear to you!"

I kept those things in the back of my mind, but I had a lot of other things happening that took much of my focus. As I grew older, for instance, I was busy excelling in school.

I graduated high school at the age of sixteen and started college when I was seventeen. As it turned out, all that time I spent at the library reading and researching and all the life lessons my parents taught me at home truly paid off. I worked extremely hard, paying my way through college and maintaining my GPA.

The years of education came and went, and before I knew it, I was buying my first house at the age of nineteen. At that point, I had a great job and a great career. I made a lot of money, I had a lot of friends, I was always outgoing and fun to be around, and I knew a lot for my age.

I was bound and determined to succeed! My parents had taught me well, and I was putting it all into practice. I was climbing the corporate ladder as fast as I could—all the way to success at the very top—and nothing was going to stop me.

I remember getting a promotion at work one year, which came with my very own office and a name plaque on the door. I was excited about it and immediately called my mom. I wanted her to see it, hoping that she would be proud of all my hard work and dedication to the things she taught me.

When I called, my mom simply said, "I'm too busy to come. I have a lot to do before your dad gets home from work."

"Sure, I get it," I replied. I did my best to understand, wishing her a good day and telling her that I loved her, even as I felt a sinking feeling of disappointment as I hung up the phone.

Next, I called my dad at his job to break the news to him. I knew that he'd be excited and would come to see me after he clocked out of work. After all, we were basically on the same side of town and only a ten-minute drive apart.

Just as I expected, my dad was ecstatic. He even left work early and came straight over. I remember him walking into my new office, looking as proud as could be.

"This is a big day for you and me both, Son," he said with the biggest grin on his face. "You did it! I'm so proud of you—and your mother will be, too!"

At that point, the smile I was wearing left my face. I told him that I had called her, but that she was just too busy to come and see me and share in my accomplishments.

My dad looked at me in compassion and said, "I'm sorry, Son. I don't understand why she has been so hard on you."

"It's okay, Dad," I responded, doing my best to shake off the disappointment. "Hey, at least you showed up!"

As I think back on that day, I remember the reason why my dad said it was a big day for both of us. He worked many long and hard years at Jeep, which paid great money and had many benefits, but he vowed never to allow any of his children to work in a factory. Instead, he told us that we were raised better than that place where he always had to punch a timecard, day in and day out.

My dad always told us, "You'll have to make it on your own."

I did just that, making him so proud of me!

At the same time, I was beginning to resent my mom. I even held animosity in my heart towards her because I felt like there wasn't anything I could do to please her, let alone make her happy.

I became cocky, arrogant, high-minded, and puffed up. My brother and two sisters still lived at home with my parents while I had already purchased my own home. I was out being my own man! I worked hard and was determined to stop at nothing to get whatever I wanted all on my own, all while my siblings seemed to always get whatever they wanted. After all, living at home had many benefits for them since my parents always took care of everything they needed and wanted.

At this time, I was married and had my first child on the way. All I seemed to do was work from sunup to sundown. On the weekends, I worked around the house. I only saw my parents now and then, but I figured that they understood that I was now a man of my own with my own responsibilities and a family to support.

Of course, my dad would often drop by to see me and ask how I was doing. I was always happy to see him. My mom, on the other hand, always seemed to be too busy to stop what she was doing and come visit. Yet, she was always sure to tell my dad to relay the message that she loved me and hoped that I was doing well.

In those days, my mom and I always seemed to clash over my priorities. I wasn't living up to her expectations. I knew that it made her sad, but my attitude wasn't helping things out at all.

In my mind, I was doing everything I could to please her, but nothing I did seemed to make her happy, let alone proud of me. In my heart, I thought that we would come to an understanding in time and would be able to talk with each other without getting into an argument. I truly hoped that better days would come. I did love my mom even if we had our differences.

After all, I was still just a young man in those days and wet behind the ears, to say the least. How much true understanding does a twenty-two-year-old really have? One thing was for certain—I had no clue how deep her love for me really went, and it took years for me to wonder about the answer before I finally came to discover the truth of the matter.

Chapter 3

The Phone Call

The afternoon of December 1, 1997, found me walking through the door of my own home after a long day at work. I could immediately tell that something was amiss, and my wife at the time soon filled me in on all the details. Apparently, my twin sister had called and told my wife off about our decision not to encourage our baby boy to call my mother "Mamma" when he grew older. Even though the two other grandchildren used that name, we felt that it would only confuse our little boy.

At that point, I did what any good husband would have done—I called my sister back and firmly requested that she respect our wishes and stay out of our business. Unfortunately, the drama was not yet over.

Several hours later, my mom called. She wasn't at all happy with me—not only about my decision to not have our son call her "Mamma" but also what I said to my sister.

No matter how I tried to explain my point of view, my mom just didn't get it.

Things turned ugly.

All that resentment I had been harboring over the years rose up inside of me. I told my mother the truth about the deep hurt I felt. I told her that I felt like she had mistreated me when I was growing up and that nothing I did would ever please her.

My mom told me point-blank that she was sorry that I felt the way I did, but the next thing she said completely shocked me.

"You are no longer my son," my mom's words came across the phone. "I wash my hands of you and I place you in God's hands."

I immediately felt a deep and sharp pain, as if my heart had been stabbed to its core and even ripped out of my chest. I thought she was done hurting me, but this was the worst yet! What could I do? Impulsively, I lashed back.

"You wash your hands of me?!" I yelled over the phone, repeating her words back to her in anger and disbelief. "You place me in God's hands?! I'm no longer your son?!"

I had to really make sure she got it. I didn't want any chance that she misunderstood me on this one! I opened my mouth in one last shout of pain and fury, words that I will never forget.

"I AM YOUR F—ING SON!! F— you, you f—ing b—!"

I had spoken my piece, so I immediately ended the call by hanging up on her and left it at that.

What I didn't know at that moment was that only several short hours later, I would receive a phone call from my sister-in-law informing me that my mom was being rushed to the hospital in an ambulance. She had been in the bathroom, getting ready for a doctor's appointment, when she suddenly collapsed.

I instantly left work, jumped in my truck, and drove to the hospital, flying down the expressway as fast as I possibly could. I had to get to my mom! So many thoughts were rushing through my mind, but mostly the last words I said to her during the previous night's conversation.

When I arrived at the hospital and urgently requested to see my mother, I was led down a series of hallways by the chief doctor on that shift. As we swiftly made our way through the corridors, the doctor explained that my mother had suffered a brain aneurysm and was a very sick lady. They were just beginning to run tests on her.

As soon as I arrived at the room, I ran to my mom's bedside, trying to throw myself into her arms. I felt hot tears of desperation falling from my eyes as I tried to get through to her.

"Mom, I'm so sorry," I cried, holding onto her. "MOM!" I continued, staring down in terror at her unresponsive face.

"Please forgive me, Mom!" I shouted even louder. I needed her to understand how sorry I was for my cruel words, my cries turning into muffled screams of anguish. "MOM, NO!! Please come back!!!"

I was too late. My mom had already passed away, and her spirit had left her body.

In that moment of torment, I remember looking around frantically for help, but only saw my dad standing there, holding the rest of the family back to allow me that last moment with her.

The date was December 2nd, my mom was forty-one, and I was only twenty-one when I lost her.

As the testing would later reveal, my mother's entire body was consumed from head to toe with leukemia. This news took us all by shock, especially because my mom's mother had lost the fight to leukemia some years back, but we had all been told that any genetic effects would skip a generation.

Speaking of my grandmother, she was an amazing woman, and both my mother and I were extremely close to her. When I was a young boy, I spent as much time with her as I could.

Meemaw was originally from Spain, a true beauty with jet-black hair, lovely blue eyes, and a pale complexion. She hardly spoke any English at all, but she mixed the two languages together the best that she could.

Of course, I could understand her perfectly. I believe that everyone can understand the language of love, and that was the most powerful thing about Meemaw—she was full of love!

Meemaw loved being with me and always made it known to the whole family that I was her favorite. She also loved to cook and could always be found in the kitchen, her apron tied around her waist and her little hands flying around busily as she made homemade tortillas, deep-fried empanadas, and fresh tamales—basically, everything that we loved to eat!

My grandmother always kept me by her side as she worked, teaching me how to roll out tortillas and showing me how to pick the freshest tomatoes and peppers from her garden. Meemaw always had such a joy about her as she spoke to me as a youngster. Like many others, she told me that she saw something special in my eyes. She just knew that one day, I would do great things.

The day that my grandmother passed was very hard on me. She was in the hospital's intensive care unit, which meant that I had to stay in the waiting room because children under a certain age were not permitted into the ICU.

Knowing that she was dying, my grandmother was determined to see me one last time. The staff would only allow it from a distance, so my father came to get me. As we walked down the hallway, he explained that I couldn't go inside the room but that he was going to pick me up so I could see Meemaw through the window.

I remember gazing through the glass that separated my grandmother and me, seeing my mom sitting next to the bed with tears in her eyes. My dad tapped on the window with his free hand to let my grandmother know I was there.

Meemaw slowly raised her eyes to see me looking in on her and gave me a tired smile. I felt sad, remembering how she had once been so full of life and now looked weak and fragile.

Meemaw continued to smile and lifted her hand ever so gently to wave me goodbye, mouthing the words, "I love you, *mijo*," before blowing me one last kiss.

Then, her hand fell weakly back on the bed, and her head dropped onto the pillow. Meemaw passed away, and her spirit left her body.

In the months that followed, my mother took Meemaw's death extremely hard and slipped into a depression that seemed to last for a very long time. She eventually came out of that time of grieving as a much stronger woman than she had been before.

Yet, even remembering and knowing all of those things didn't help me with the pain I was feeling at the time of my own mother's passing.

I remember looking around at my brother and sisters as we all stood in that hospital room, total shock and disbelief showing on our faces to reflect the deep heartbreak that we were feeling. How could this really be happening?

Then there was my father, always bringing such a glow with him and sharing his happiness with everyone he met—now feeling utterly hollow and appearing like a shell of a man. He did his best to hold back his tears when he was in front of us, but there was no hiding the great pain he was feeling.

My dad looked as if his life had been ripped away from him and was now over. He deeply loved my mother, and she loved him. After all, they had been soulmates and enjoyed twenty-six years of marriage—growing together, nurturing a family together, building a home together, and living life together. All of that had been torn away in the blink of an eye.

Over the next three days, many things transpired as if in a whirlwind—my mom's showing, her funeral, so many family members and friends gathering to say their final goodbyes, and more. As each day passed, the reality of her death sank in a little bit more. As many expressed, her passing was such a great loss to the faith and was felt by many on that tragic day of December 2, 1997.

As all these things were taking place, I had unknowingly shouldered a Cross of Deep Regret, a heavy burden that bent my back from the weight and turned my face to the ground. In the days and nights that followed, this cross went with me wherever I traveled, adding more weight to my already troubled mind and heaping more shame upon my sorely aching heart.

I remember standing next to my father at the funeral home when he turned to me. In his own sorrow, he was determined to check on me.

"Donnie, how are you doing?" he asked in his loving way. "I know you and your mother had your differences, and she was so hard on you, but I want you to know that she always loved you."

I gave his words some space for a moment and then simply responded with a shrug. "I'm okay. Just holding it together—just like you." I had always wanted to be like my dad, after all.

My dad thought about that for a moment and then tried a different approach. "I haven't seen you cry yet, Donnie. I believe it's my fault."

He went on to say something that completely floored me.

"I've raised you to believe that men don't cry, and I'm sorry for saying that because it's anything but the truth." My dad went on to explain how he often took his own time to cry, asking if I remembered all of the times he jumped in his truck and went for a ride on his own.

I remembered the times I had asked to go along with him, but he told me that I would have to wait for another time.

"Those were the times I needed to just be alone with my own thoughts—to pray, to talk with the Lord, and, yes, to cry," my dad clarified.

Honestly, I couldn't believe what I was hearing. "MY dad cries?!" I struggled to understand as my thoughts swirled together. "MY dad has to get away and be alone at times because HIS life felt overwhelming?!"

My dad wasn't finished. "You have to just let it out, Son. Tears bring healing," he said. "You can't hold it in and bottle it up forever—it will only destroy you!"

At that point, I thought that maybe my dad was just saying all of this to help me cope. After all, he and I both knew what a strong person I was and how I always put my feelings aside to be strong for others.

In the days that followed, I thought deeply about my dad's words of wisdom, but I never acted on it. In fact, I couldn't cry. The tears just wouldn't come! I couldn't explain exactly why, but part of it was because I just felt like I couldn't show any weakness. All eyes were on me, and others were drawing strength off of me. How could I let them down?

As my father mourned the loss of my mother, I remember wrapping my arms around him at different points. I wanted to take his pain away, I wanted to shield him from the hurt he was feeling, I wanted to protect him from a bleak future without her. What more could I do except what I was already doing? Worst of all, I was left feeling that our loss would have serious repercussions.

On our way to the cemetery, my dad knew that something more than my mom's death was bothering me. So, he asked me what it was.

I was reluctant to tell him, especially since he was already dealing with so much.

Nonetheless, because my dad and I shared everything with each other, he pressed me, telling me to hold nothing back. We were that close.

Finally, I told him what had taken place earlier that morning, just before I had left my house for the funeral home. It had shaken me up and angered me.

What happened was that I received a call from my uncle—my dad's brother—who told me that he had called a psychic. Apparently, she had informed my uncle that my dad was going to commit suicide as a result of my mom's passing.

When my dad heard this, he was enraged! I knew just as well as he did—calling on a psychic or seeking out a familiar spirit was something that simply was not done in our household. It went against everything we believed in!

My dad immediately called his brother and told him that he was not welcome at my mom's burial. Furthermore, my dad had some very choice words for his brother.

"How dare you call my son on the very morning that he is going to bury his mother! How dare you say such a horrible thing about me on the very day I'm going to bury my wife!"

I finally calmed my dad down and we reached the funeral home in one piece after that miserable debacle.

The rest of that day, we proceeded to lay my mother to rest. It was the hardest thing we ever had to do together, and most of all for my dad who had to leave behind his one true love to be covered in dirt. Never again would he be able to see her, hold her, kiss her, or converse with her like he did every day for the last twenty-six years. As if that were not enough, now he had his children to think about and care for—young adults who were now without a mother.

In the days ahead, I had my own hurt to deal with. As I thought about my mom, the memories brought me great regret—the disrespect I unleashed on her, my selfish desire to become someone of stature, my time wasted on fruitless things when I could have spent valuable time learning from her. All of it had led me down the wrong path and caused me great internal pain to remember it.

If only I had done things differently! After all, I always loved my mother, always sought her approval, and always wanted her to be proud of me and my many accomplishments. I wanted nothing more than for her to see how the son she raised was becoming a man, and not just any man but a true man of integrity. After all, I was her oldest son, and she had the greatest of hopes for me.

Each time I took a moment to face reality, I knew that I was not at all the man that my mom desired me to be. Worse than that, I was not at all the man that God intended me to be.

In the years that followed, the Cross of Deep Regret that I had unknowingly picked up after my mom's passing only proved to grow in size and in weight.

Chapter 4

Where Are You, God?

O ver the next three years, I watched my father steadily decline. Every ounce of his natural happiness and hope was gone, resulting in him being lost and broken in the deepest way imaginable.

My dad's deterioration was extremely painful for me to watch. My father was my best friend, the greatest dad that any boy could ever wish for. I always looked up to him, and he has always been my true hero.

When I was growing up as a small boy, I was his little shadow. Wherever my dad was, there I was. Everyone in the family called him "Uncle Donnie," so I decided that my name was "Uncle Donnie," too. After all, I was named after him!

My father taught me so many things, especially how to be there for others. He was so full of love and compassion. He was the guy who would literally give you the shirt off his back, stopping at nothing to help others out. To me, his actions were a true testimony to the kind of man that he was.

My dad's compassionate nature grew out of a very abusive childhood. His father, my grandfather, had many unresolved issues that resulted in him being cold, bitter, and ruthless, even toward his own family. My grandfather beat my father all the time, even to the point of kicking him with steel-toed boots when my father fell to the ground and tried to hide under the kitchen table to avoid further blows. I always remember how my dad slept with his hands over his head, even as an adult. He was never able to get rid of his built-in fear that he was going to get beat up in his sleep.

As a young child, my dad swore that he would never treat his own children the same way his father treated him. He kept that promise, going to great lengths to ensure we always felt loved and cherished.

Ironically, despite the terrible stories I heard about my grandfather, I came to know a very different person. Don't get me wrong—the stories my dad told me about his upbringing were all true, but my relationship with my grandfather left others amazed. The only way I can explain this is to say that while my grandfather was busy shutting out everyone in his life and keeping them away from him, he was drawn to me.

Grandpa was a retired Vietnam vet, having contracted gangrene and being exposed to Agent Orange during his tours. His health was suffering— he lived off of an oxygen tank, he had a colostomy bag, and he was down to only half a lung. Cancer was eating him alive.

Although my father had terrible memories of his childhood, he always went by his parents' house once a week to check on them, bring them groceries, and see if there was anything at their house that needed attention.

It was during these weekly trips that I spent time with my grandfather. I sat on his lap and listened to his old eight-track tapes. He especially loved the old country gospel hymns because they brought him peace. He told me all kinds of stories about the artists—Bill Monroe, Johnny Cash, Patsy Cline, Waylon Jennings, and others. I enjoyed learning all about them and still like listening to them today.

Grandpa also loved to tell me about his war stories and the friends he made while he traveled the world. He did some pretty amazing things and had plenty of medals to prove it. At one point, I even knew what every medal represented and why he received them. He was a highly decorated officer, which made me think that even though my grandfather did a lot of horrible things, he also did a lot of good so that had to count for something.

Personally, I felt that his fight to stay alive had gotten the best of him after living such an adventurous life. Grandpa was now bound to his bed, barely able to walk because it took too much effort and caused him to gasp for a breath of air.

We even tried not to laugh very much when we talked since it would take a lot of his energy. In fact, many of our visits ended with Grandpa becoming very tired and falling asleep.

Before I knew it, my dad was peeking into the room and nodding at me that it was time to go.

"I love you, Grandpa," I whispered. "I'll be back later."

I even found myself at his bedside when he passed. I was still young, so I was cuddled up next to him. His arm was around me, tucking me in close in the same way we always sat and talked.

Grandpa looked up at my dad who sat nearby. "Don't worry," my grandfather said with a peaceful smile. "I see Jesus standing at the door!"

Just moments later, Grandpa gave up his last breath and his spirit passed from his body.

My grandfather was honored by the U.S. military on the day of his funeral. An American flag covered his casket, a seven-man firing squad fired off three shots, and a bugler even played "Taps." After the officers gave a formal salute, the flag was carefully folded and presented to my family.

Once a decorated war hero, my grandfather had officially finished the journey of life. I felt proud of who he was and what he fought for—he didn't only fight to live in his latter days but also fought for his country and the lives of so many others.

No matter what anybody else thought about him, I decided that other people's opinions were not going to change my thinking about him. After all, he was my dad's father, and without him, I wouldn't have my dad. At the very least, I owed him that much, as my father was the greatest man I have ever known.

Don't get me wrong—my father was not a perfect man. He had many struggles to overcome due to his hurt, pain, and lack of a safe childhood home, including drug addiction and rage. As he grew up, began learning life lessons from the School of Hard Knocks, and married my mother, there were many things that he had to deal with head-on.

My mom had a lot to do with my dad's healing process, as she was the first one to get saved in their new household. As the story goes, they were already married, and my mother was sixteen. She and some friends decided to fool around with a wooden Ouija board, thinking that it was just an innocent game.

After all, my mother didn't believe what others had told her about the board, so she was determined to find the truth out for herself.

So, my mother asked the Ouija board a serious question about her life. Whatever answer returned to my mom was enough to frighten her into throwing it out. To her surprise, however, no matter how many times she threw that board in the trash, it somehow wound up back in her house.

Not knowing what else to do, my mother told my father about her dilemma, and together they decided to take the wooden board out back and burn it. After several attempts with no success, the board finally caught fire all of a sudden and turned completely to ash. My mother vowed never to touch or play with a Ouija board ever again.

I have no idea what question my mom asked the board and what answer was given, as she was careful never to talk about those details. What I do know, however, is that the experience was enough to prompt my mom to look for serious answers to spiritual questions.

In her research, she came to understand the power of good and evil, which changed her life forever. At that point, my mother gave her life to the Lord and became a prayer warrior, not only for her own life but for the lives of many others.

Her first prayer was for my dad. She began to pray day and night that he would also find peace, safety, and security in the Lord. After all, my mother dearly loved my father with her whole heart, so she did not think it strange to beseech the Lord on his behalf, often in tears and sometimes even fasting for his salvation.

Years of praying went by. My dad had not changed, but my mom had not given up.

One Sunday, my dad decided to attend a church meeting with us. As skeptical as he was about "religion," he wanted to support my mom. He saw himself as the head of the household, and after all, he loved his family dearly.

During that meeting, my dad suddenly felt called to go up to the front of the building and kneel down at the altar. He didn't feel this way because an altar call had been given, for it was during the middle of the sermon.

Ignoring everyone else, my dad got up from his seat, walked up to the altar, knelt down, and began to weep. Mind you, I was a small boy at that time and had never seen my dad cry before, let alone weep! The Lord had been working on my dad's heart all along, calling him to come to Him.

The prayers of my mother were being answered! That very same day, my dad asked the Lord into his life and into his heart as his own Lord and Savior. A true conversion took place, and my father came home a new man.

The addiction to drugs? They were GONE! The anger and occasional rages? GONE! The hurt he experienced as a child? GONE!

Instead, there stood in our home a new man—a man of peace who was gentle, loving, kind, and compassionate! Most amazing of all was that it was like my dad had received a double portion of all these gifts because his mere presence could now be felt wherever he went.

After my mom's death, my father made another dramatic change, but this was not for the better. He was a whole different man—broken, lost, no place to go, nowhere to hide, and no one to run home to. The loss of my mother was more than he could bear.

It was not long before my dad began to seriously contemplate suicide. Throughout it all, I was there for him—someone he loved and trusted, someone to listen to his hurt and pain, someone who heard his private thoughts of ending his very own life.

Can you imagine what it must be like to hear someone whom you truly love, adore, and idolize speak like this, let alone your very own father? His was not a selfish cry for attention or a frightened cry for help. My dad's pain was deep, and it was real.

My mother could never be replaced, and the void caused by her death could never be filled.

I was twenty-five years old at the time and all I wanted to do was save my dad from the destructive downward spiral that he was on. I hugged him, I held him, I told him how much he meant to me, and I explained how much I looked up to him. I even told him that he was my hero, and I begged him not to leave me.

Unfortunately, my father had already attempted suicide two times, each time being a near miss that made me even more concerned and protective of him.

In response, my dad sought help from his doctor and accepted the medical care that was provided to him, spending time in various mental health facilities. Every day when I spoke with him, he told me how much he missed my mother. As each year passed, certain dates—her birthday, holidays, their anniversary, and the day of her death—only seemed to make it more difficult for him, haunting his every waking moment.

I could only imagine the internal struggle that he was constantly dealing with. On the one hand, he wanted my mother back and longed for the life that he had known with her in it. On the other hand, my dad bravely faced the reality of knowing that the love of his life was gone and would never come back, all while seeing that he had a motherless son who loved him dearly and needed him desperately.

Surely, this place of crisis was a terrible one to be in and a dreadful one to face every day. As the battle within my dad only grew worse, the days ahead seemed increasingly hopeless and cold. He spent every day at her place of rest, mourning his loss.

It was like he was forced to wake up every morning and feel the same agonizing chill in his bones, knowing that he would never again feel the warmth of my mother's love. Not only that, but he recognized that no one else could provide him with the same fulfilling love that she gave him.

As for the dreams that my dad and my mom shared for the future? Those were gone forever. In short, my dad now knew what life looked like without my mom, and he wanted no part of it.

Death can be a terrible thing for the living who are left behind—suffering great loss, trying to cope, and learning how to grieve. I personally did not find much comfort in the grieving process, so I looked for other ways to numb the pain and hurt. Cocaine and alcohol, for example, is what I went to for a quick fix.

I soon realized, however, that those things were inadequate. The drug-induced numbness wore off far too quickly, and the alcohol left me with a hangover that was less than desirable. Meanwhile, I was left facing the loss and the hurt all over again. Wasn't there anything that would take it away?!

All I could think in the midst of my internal conflict was to go over the facts again and again and again—my mother was gone, and my father whom I loved deeply was self-destructing before my very eyes. No matter how hard I tried to do something about those external factors, I just couldn't fix it, let alone the things that were taking place inside of me and within my own life.

Sure, on the outside, I appeared to have it all together. I'd smile, crack jokes, hang out with my friends, and make it to work every day.

All the while, that which was most important to me in the whole entire world—my beloved father— was crumbling beneath my feet. There wasn't a thing I could do to stop it, and that was not only breaking my heart but crushing me to my very core!

That Cross of Deep Regret that I had been unknowingly carrying around only continued to grow, now with added layers of depression, deep despair, and grief. It was an awful burden to shoulder.

In the midst of all of this turmoil, I remember asking, "God, are You seeing any of this? Do You even care? Where are You, God?! Why, in the middle of my and my father's great suffering, have You decided to go silent on us?!"

That was the worst part of it—I didn't know if my grief-filled questions were making it any higher than the ceiling. Yet, I was determined to get to the bottom of it. I had to know the truth.

Little did I know at the time, my quest in search of truth would prove to be extremely painful. In fact, relentless, as this was only the beginning of the hurt that I was already enduring. Nothing, and I mean nothing, could have ever prepared me for what came next.

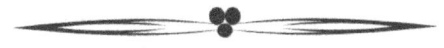

Chapter 5

The Letter and the Poem

By the end of August 2001, my father had reached the point where he needed to spend a whole week in the mental ward. While he was there, I went to see him every single day during visiting hours. It was very difficult to see him in that place, away from the people he loved and surrounded by others who suffered from mental illnesses.

My dad was strong, gentle-hearted, and hardworking, having only two years left in Jeep before his retirement. He was successful in all he did, devoted to his family and friends, and compassionate toward those who were unable to look after themselves. My dad spent many days reaching the lost, feeding the homeless, and caring for the widows. He had such a passion to reach the hearts of others.

On one particular afternoon, I went to see my dad as usual, and we began to talk about what was taking place inside the mental ward. My dad told me that he couldn't believe that he was seeing some of the things that were actually taking place while he was in there.

As I listened to him explain, I hoped that maybe, just maybe, he had seen just enough to shake him from his thoughts of self-destruction. I also hoped that my dad had taken the time to encourage other people that he saw on a daily basis, maybe even meeting others who had a similar story to his.

Unfortunately, he was in a very dark place and didn't have it in him to minister to others. The loving and compassionate part of him that was always looking out for others had been buried beneath layers of deep despair, pain, and agony.

My dad looked at me and grabbed my hand. He told me, "Donnie, you have to get me out of here. I'm not crazy! I'm hurt and I'm broken with good reason, and there's a difference."

At that point, I asked him if he had mingled with the other people or had spoken to any of them.

My dad immediately saw what I was driving at and shook his head. "No, they're too medicated to understand anything," he explained. "When they look at me, it's like they're lost in space or something."

I nodded in understanding, not having much faith in the so-called mental health system anyway. A bit tongue-in-cheek, I asked him how his therapy sessions were coming along and what the doctor had said about the rehabilitation program he had been assigned to attend.

My dad told me how the psychiatrists wanted to put him on pills, going on to explain that no matter how he tried to share his thoughts and feelings, there was no way that any of them could truly understand what he was going through.

"You're the only one who gets me, Donnie," he said to me, gripping my arm again. "You know how close me and your mom were. You know what our life was about and what it was like."

My dad went on to talk more about the lack of compassion and true understanding in that facility. "I feel like I'm a bug stuck in a jar or something," he admitted, explaining that he was often treated like a research project or science experiment by the attending physicians. None of them showed the slightest bit of understanding about what he was really going through.

Speaking of practitioners, my dad told me that he had an appointment with the doctor later that day.

"I'm going to have him call you," he began as he outlined his plan to get out of that place. His idea was to tell the doctor that he was doing much better now and felt ready to check out and go home.

As I listened to his plan, I understood that my dad wanted me to tell the doctor about our visit and how I also felt that he was doing much better. My dad even suggested that I tell the doctor that his latest suicide attempt had simply been caused by the thoughts of the upcoming holidays.

"Tell him that it won't happen again and that all I need to get my life back in order is to be with you, Donnie. Tell him that. If I'm with you, then I'll be able to get everything back on track."

I looked at my dad for a moment, mulling over everything that he had just relayed to me. I could see that he was still waiting for me to confirm that I was going to convince the doctor that my dad was going to be fine as long as he was with me.

"Dad," I said, "I need you to make me a promise." I began to tell him how I needed to know that his attempts to end his life were over. It was one thing to convince a doctor that he was going to be all right, but I needed to know for myself. I didn't have that assurance yet, but I wanted more than anything to feel at peace.

"I have to know that no matter how hard things get in the future that we're going to stick it out together," I told my dad, blinking away tears as I gazed at him. "You and me, Dad, we can get through this together—through thick and thin—I just know it. But I need to hear you say it."

More than anything, I needed my dad to tell me himself that I wasn't going to receive yet another phone call from an intervention officer or a mental illness physician. My deepest fear was that as much as my dad talked optimistically about turning a corner or making a positive change, he was just saying that to get out of the mental health ward. Honestly, deep down inside, I feared the worst.

My dad looked at me straight in the eyes and grabbed my hand. "I love you, Donnie," he said, his voice firm. "I promise that you and I will see this through. You have my word on this!"

At that, I felt the first little spark of hope returning to me. After all, in my house growing up, giving someone our WORD meant everything. We also had this saying that went right along with it. "Say what you mean, mean what you say, and do what you say you're going to do." This was our own definition of what it meant to be a man of integrity.

The visit was swiftly coming to a close, so we hugged goodbye, both of us unable to hold back the tears. I was certain that my dad's plan to get out of there would work, and I already knew my talk with the doctor would be a big part of it.

Yet, my dad reminded me to stay by the phone so I wouldn't miss the physician's call. I could tell he was eager to get out of there, so I assured him that I would tell the doctor everything we had discussed.

"Don't worry, Dad," I said as I headed out the door. "I'll see you soon." I knew that I'd be back to pick him up just as soon as the doctor released him.

When the doctor called, he informed me that he had met with my father and was currently working on filling out the discharge paperwork.

I took the opportunity to ask the doctor his professional opinion. "How do you think my dad is doing?"

The doctor replied that he felt as if my dad was doing much better. "Of course, he'll only continue to improve once he's safely home and surrounded by loved ones," he assured me.

Then the doctor asked me what I thought, and I told him that I agreed with him. I did my best to sound positive and affirming, which was just what my dad had asked me to do.

After that, the doctor went over the discharge rules with me. I listened carefully to each and every one—

First, my dad was being released under my supervision, which meant that he would be staying with me at my place for the next four weeks.

Next, my dad had to make every appointment with his personal physician, a man who was a good friend of the family and a psychiatrist to boot.

Finally, my dad was not allowed to drink any alcohol while taking his prescribed medication.

From there, all that was left to be done was for me to sign off on the discharge paperwork, thereby agreeing to all of the terms set forth, and pick my dad up at 11:00 PM.

I was happy to return to the hospital to pick up my dad. As I went in to sign the necessary forms, I could see him waiting for me, an eager look in his eyes, as if he was just aching to get out of there.

Once I was finished with the formalities, my dad greeted me with a hug.

"Where are ya parked?" he asked, shouldering his small bag and following me out to the parking lot. He was happy to get into my truck and take the short drive back to my place.

It was nearly midnight when we arrived at my house. The night air was mild, but it held a slight chill, a warning that fall was on its way and the brutal cold of winter would soon follow. I felt the same way—even though everything seemed calm and hopeful with my dad's return home on the outside, there was still a relentless fear pricking me and giving me a sick feeling in the pit of my stomach.

My dad was obviously extremely exhausted, yet happy to tell me how relieved he was to be out of that place and finally be home with me.

In turn, I told him how happy I was to have him home. "Everything from here on out is going to be okay," I assured him, the tears immediately springing into my eyes as I spoke words that I did not quite feel.

"After all, we have each other," I said.

Remembering his words from earlier in the day, I once again made him promise me that he would not attempt to end his life. Still crying, I felt terrified that the nightmare wasn't over just yet, but I didn't want my dad to know exactly what I was feeling. My trust in his future actions had already been lost.

My dad came up to me and gave me a reassuring hug. "I love you, Donnie," he told me. "I promise you—trust me on this—everything's going to be all right."

At that, there wasn't anything else left to say. I brought my dad to his room, showing him where to find fresh, clean towels so he could take a nice, hot shower.

"I'll be making you something to eat," I told him. At that, I gently closed the bedroom door and headed back to the kitchen.

Just before I got started, I reached for my trusty stash of cocaine that I kept hidden away in the cabinets. I quickly drew a few lines and snorted them up to calm myself down before wiping off the counter and getting started on dinner.

When my dad came down, we sat at the table, and we ate and talked—or I should say that he ate and talked while I sat and listened. I was simply happy to have him back home with me.

By that point, it was very late and far past midnight. My dad had plans in the morning to head out of town to see his sister and her kids for the day since he was extremely close to her and hadn't seen her in a while. So, as soon as he finished eating, it was off to bed for him so he could be early to rise, as was his habit.

Just before my dad said goodnight to me, he looked at me and told me something that shocked me.

"Oh, by the way, Son? That stuff you just put up your nose isn't good for you." His words were gentle, but they packed a punch. "I raised you much better than that. Plus, it's a waste of an honest man's wage."

With that, my dad gave me a great big hug, kissed me on the cheek, and held me tight for another moment as he said, "I love you. I'll see you in the morning."

After my dad assured me once again that everything was going to be all right and went up the stairs to his room, I stared after him for a minute longer. I couldn't believe that he knew about my self-medication! After all, I thought I had kept it a secret.

Feeling shame and embarrassment wash over me, I returned to my own room, thinking that I had totally let my dad down. I wanted to fix the whole situation, but I didn't know how to approach it. I mulled over everything in my mind that night before falling asleep, but the subject was never brought up again.

The next morning, my dad and I had our coffee together before we headed off in different directions—he went on his trip out of town to see his sister, nieces, and nephews while I went to hang out with a young boy who needed a man in his life.

I remember feeling like everything in the world was going to be okay, even while I was still a hot mess at the time. I was glad that my dad would be spending time with family and that I was able to be a mentor to a kid who looked up to me and desperately needed a role model.

That whole day, I kept thinking about my dad and how I was looking forward to going home at the end of the day to spend time with him. I was excited just imagining how I would get to ask him how his trip went and how the family was doing. More than anything, I had wanted to go with my dad for his trip out of town, but since I had already given my word to the little guy that we would be spending the day together, I couldn't let him down by suddenly changing my plans.

The day came and went, and I was glad to spend the day with that young boy. We had a lot of fun together, first playing putt-putt and then hanging out at the park.

I didn't get home until late, sometime after 8:00 PM. I noticed that my dad wasn't back yet as I arrived, but I fully expected him to walk in the door at any moment since I knew he liked to be in bed by 10:00 PM at the latest.

Another thing I immediately noticed when I walked in was that my answering machine had a lot of messages—over thirty, in fact, which struck me as very odd.

"That must be wrong," I thought as I looked at the missed call count in confusion. "No one ever calls me like that!"

I proceeded to check the messages and soon discovered that there was no mistake. A slow, creeping panic came over me as I filtered through dozens of voicemails from the last several hours, with the first ones coming in shortly after 3:00 PM.

The messages were all left by official people with urgent voices from various emergency services—the sheriff's department, local law enforcement, and hospital staff. All the while, a warning bell was sounding in the back of my mind that my dad still wasn't home yet.

As I grabbed a nearby pad and pencil to jot down the return numbers, my mind was racing to make sense of everything.

"Oh my God," I thought. "Has Dad been in an accident?! Did he swerve into oncoming traffic in another attempt to take his life?!"

I knew exactly what roads he would have taken to go see his sister, and I knew them well. My dad always loved taking the backroads—mostly old truckers' routes—and enjoyed rambling drives through the countryside. He often took those roads when he needed to get away and recharge, and he taught me to love them as well when he taught me how to drive.

With all this in mind, I called the first number I scribbled down, which was for the sheriff's department. As soon as the officer on duty picked up, I told him who I was and about the many messages I had received from their office.

While he wasn't able to tell me anything, he immediately transferred me to the hospital's special care unit for an update.

I waited impatiently as the phone began to ring all over again, the questions already flying through my mind.

"What's going on?" I asked as soon as the first nurse picked up the phone. "Is my dad all right?"

As it turned out, she was in charge of my dad's care and was not allowed to tell anyone else what was going on except for me. So, she started by asking me a series of very personal questions to make sure I was who I said I was.

After successfully verifying my identity, the nurse informed me that my father had been in a serious accident and was in critical condition.

This was the worst possible answer. I dropped the phone, jumped in my truck, and drove to the hospital as fast as I could. As I flew down the highway, I had flashbacks about the same kind of frantic drive to the hospital for my mom. I could only desperately hope for a very different outcome, as I had finally just brought him home that previous night.

When I arrived, I was directed to the special care unit, a very private wing that few hospital visitors even knew existed.

I was greeted at the door of the special care unit by the very same nurse who spoke with me on the phone. She was taking care of my father and had more screening questions for me before she was able to explain to me what had happened.

Even though she prewarned me in the kindest way possible about what she was going to tell me and what I was about to see, there was nothing that could have ever truly prepared me for the next few moments of my life.

The nurse told me that my father had put a .25 caliber pistol into his mouth and pulled the trigger. He was found at the same cemetery where his father was buried, about thirty yards from my grandfather's gravesite. He had been locked inside his truck with his head slumped over the steering wheel.

She went on to explain to me all of the life-saving measures that had been taken up to this point to save my dad's life—he was life-flighted to the hospital, he was hooked up to a ventilator to keep him alive because he could no longer breathe on his own, and he was monitored very closely to remain stable.

The nurse told me that they would be running one more test in the next few hours to determine if my dad had any more brain activity. If he had none, he would remain in a vegetative state for the rest of his life. At that point, I would be given one of two choices—one, keep him on the ventilator and have him fed through a tube, or two, shut him off and allow him to go peacefully.

"Are you ready to see him?" the nurse asked me, having told me everything there was to say.

I told her that I was ready, but I still had no idea what I would be walking into.

The nurse walked me to the entrance of my dad's room and then faced me for a moment, placing her hands on my shoulders and saying gently, "I'll leave you two alone for a while. If you need anything, I'll be right out here."

There was nothing more for me to do but to quietly walk through the door to see my dad. It was a rather large room that was dimly lit and felt very cold. There were only two small lights on, one on each side of his bed.

As I walked slowly toward my dad's bedside, I felt my heart tearing apart to see him laid out on the hospital bed, still and motionless, save for the machines that were keeping him alive. My eyes were immediately drawn to his hands because they were covered in brown paper bags, which I later learned was because of the gunpowder residue that was left on them in the aftermath.

I felt my lips begin to tremble as I sank into the chair beside his bed and asked through the blinding tears, "Dad, what did you do?" My voice barely above a whisper, I pressed him again, "What did you do, Dad?"

As I said that, his head slowly moved to the side and fell gently onto his shoulder. I stared at his head for just a second, clearly seeing the exit wound in the back of his head where the bullet had passed through. Rising swiftly, I gently repositioned my dad's head by softly replacing it on the pillow where it had previously rested.

In my heart, I knew that my dad had waited for me to get there, but it did not relieve the thousands of questions that were flashing through my mind. Questions like "What happens next?" and "Who should I call?"

Then there were the deeper questions that I would have to address later like "What really happened?" and "How could Dad do this to me?" I knew there had to be more information about the whole situation than what I had initially been given.

I sat beside my dad for the longest time, my head resting in the middle of his chest and listening to his still-beating heart. It felt comforting to be with him, even though the questions continued to swirl, the tears continued to flow, and the situation was far too dreadful for me to feel any peace.

After what seemed like forever, I got up and kissed him on his cheek.

"I'll be right back, Dad," I told him. "Don't worry—I'm not leaving you."

I studied his face for a moment longer, wondering if he could still hear me.

Taking a deep breath, I did my best to compose myself. I wiped the tears from my eyes and headed back to the nurses' station, looking for the nurse assigned to my dad.

She was there, waiting for me with a kind and compassionate look on her face. As I began to pepper her with questions, she patiently began to answer everything to the best of her knowledge.

My first question was if anyone else had been notified because I knew my dad had been in the hospital since 3:00 PM. By now, it was well after 9:00 PM and I was a bit surprised to not see any friends or family there.

The nurse replied, "No, you are the only person permitted to be here."

My face immediately registered confusion, so she quickly put her hand up, motioning for me to wait a second as she retrieved an evidence bag from the desk. I looked on as she pulled a piece of paper from the file and handed it to me.

As I quickly discovered, the paper was a letter that my dad had written from his truck, addressing it to whoever would find him—and me.

"In case of an emergency," said the letter, "please contact ONLY my son, Donnie. Allow no visitors until he arrives. He will know exactly what to do."

My mind and heart began reeling in pain again, but my dad was not finished writing.

"Donnie, if you're reading this, I am sorry for leaving you. Know in your heart that I love you and am now in a better place with your mother. We are just fine, and I'm sorry."

I wanted to get away and sit down somewhere, but there was more.

The nurse was pulling out another piece of paper from her evidence bag and handing it to me. She explained that this had also been in my father's truck when he had been rescued. It was found in his lap, to be exact.

I took it from the nurse and gazed at it, seeing familiar words to a famous poem. Tears began to prick the corners of my eyes as I realized that my dad's blood was splattered across it and that it was most likely the last thing his eyes saw before he pulled the trigger.

The poem was by Margaret Fishback Powers and read as follows:

One night, I had a dream–

I dreamed I was walking along the beach

With the Lord,

And across the sky, flashed scenes from my life.

For each scene, I noticed two sets of footprints

In the sand—

One belonged to me and the other to the Lord.

When the last scene of my life flashed before me,

I looked back at the footsteps in the sand.

I noticed that many times along the path of my life,

There was only one set of footprints.

I also noticed that it happened at the very lowest

And saddest times in my life.

This really bothered me,

And I questioned the Lord about it.

"Lord, You said that once I decided to follow You,

You would walk with me all the way,

But I have noticed that during

The most troublesome times in my life

There is only one set of footprints.

I don't understand why

In times when I needed You most,

You should leave me."

The Lord replied, "My precious, precious child,

I love you and I would never leave you

During your times of trial and suffering.

When you saw only one set of footprints,

It was then that I carried you."

As I finished the poem, the tears started to run in rivers down my face. It was too much for me to bear.

"Come here, dear child," I heard the nurse's voice. She swiftly walked around the desk to put her arms around me. She was just in time, too, because I felt my knees giving way and thought I was going to faint or collapse.

To my surprise, this frail little woman held me up on my feet as the sobs shook my shoulders. She brought comfort to me, being in many ways my angel in time of desperate need.

For the next few hours, I had phone calls to make and directions to give. One person I called was my uncle, my dad's brother and the one who had called the psychic after my mom's death. I wanted to let him know that his brother had passed and how it happened.

I also spent a lot of time sitting alone with my dad in his hospital room, painful questions coursing through my mind as I sat waiting for the results of his brain tests.

"Why, Dad?"

"Was my love not strong enough for you?"

"Whatever happened to 'Everything is going to be all right'?"

I felt completely empty on the inside and totally numb on the outside. I was in total shock, desperately wanting to suddenly wake up from this horrible nightmare to find myself back at my house with my dad, both of us safe and sound and enjoying each other's company. Instead, I was fighting with everything I had in me to stay strong and not completely lose it.

The test results finally came back. My dad had no brain activity, which meant that he was legally brain-dead. At that point, it was my call to make the medical decision—keep him alive on the ventilator or let him rest in peace.

The kind nurse stood before me and my father patiently, holding two sets of paper in her hands. I was required to sign one of them. Each set determined that my dad would receive a different fate.

It was the toughest decision I had to make in my entire life. I felt sick, alone, and backed into a corner. Deep down inside, I knew exactly what I had to do, but I couldn't do it.

"Can I have a little more time?" I asked the nurse in a soft and gentle tone, looking at her without really seeing her.

She nodded with understanding and compassion as she tucked both sets of paperwork into my father's file at the foot of his bed. I needed to be alone and think this through one last time.

If I kept my dad alive, so to speak, he would never be the same. We would never talk again, and he would never walk again. He wouldn't be able to think for himself, and he wouldn't make any decisions, since he was now pronounced legally brain dead.

I knew in my heart that I had to let my dad go. My photographic memory scanned over the letter and the poem once more, and I felt a sinking feeling inside. I knew exactly what my dad wanted me to do, so I knew that I had to do it. The choice before me was clear—all I had to do was do it.

My decision was made, and it was final. I signed all of the legal documents and listened to the nurse as she went through all of the formalities with me.

I watched as the ventilator attached to my dad was shut off and unplugged. As she stood by my side, the nurse told me how the air would leave his body for the very last time.

My dad released his final breath—his upper body coming up off the bed and falling back down again as he died. It was as if he had awoken from a bad dream and then immediately had fallen back asleep. It was all over—his spirit had now left his body. He was only forty-seven when he passed.

I looked down at my dad and said quietly, "Go in peace, Dad. I will always love you. I promise to finish this and lay you to rest next to Mom—don't worry about a thing. I've got you—you have my word on this."

I leaned down to kiss his forehead and his cheek before sinking back into the chair and laying my head upon his chest for the final time. I sat lost in grief and agony in the cold silence with my dad's shell for a whole hour. I knew that the next time I saw him would be at the funeral home surrounded by many people. I just wanted to be alone and have my own personal time with him—just him and me.

The date was August 27, 2001—the longest day of my life.

I still had so many unanswered questions that I needed to sort out. I knew that I would do whatever it took to find the answers. I also was fully aware that the morning would bring many more decisions that I would have to make—a crushing load that I hardly knew how to bear.

For example, I wondered, "Why did my dad decide to take his own life at his father's cemetery, just thirty yards from his grave?" I wanted to find out the answer, but deep down inside, I knew that it was a question that only my dad could answer.

Now, it was too late to discover that mystery. My dad was no longer here to answer this question—or many others. I would simply have to come to peace without knowing that detail.

There was one other critical detail that pressed me for an answer, however. I felt that I desperately needed to know the answer to this question for my own peace of mind—"Who found my dad?"

So, as soon as morning arrived, I called the sheriff's department to find out who was in charge of the initial investigation. As I waited to be transferred to the investigator, I did my best to maintain my composure. I knew that I had to be strong and hold myself together since I was still in a state of shock and unbelief.

When the detective answered the phone, I explained who I was and what I was calling for. She was very sympathetic, telling me everything she knew and what she had found at the scene of the accident.

The detective also told me the story about how my dad had been discovered. Apparently, there was a lady who was on her way to go shopping. As she drove by the cemetery, she noticed my dad quietly sitting in his truck. She assumed he was deep in thought, just there to pay his respects to someone he had known.

After the lady went shopping, she drove back home along the same road. This time, when she passed, she noticed that my dad's truck was still there. This time, however, his head was no longer upright—it was slumped over the steering wheel.

Immediately, the lady went to check on my dad. As she approached, she knew exactly what had happened based on what she saw, so she quickly tried to open the door. She needed to check him, see if he was okay, and figure out if he still had a pulse. At that point, she discovered that he had locked himself inside. Having no way of reaching him, the lady called 911.

As I heard this story about how this woman—someone I had never met before—showed true compassion to my dad, I felt deeply touched. A sense of overwhelming gratitude washed over me and I suddenly wished to have the opportunity to meet the woman.

I instantly knew how I would respond if I ever had the chance to meet that amazing lady. I would have hugged her and thanked her from the bottom of my heart for showing such care and compassion to my father in his time of need.

What a strong and courageous person she was! Let's face it—how many people are truly bold and caring enough to willingly walk into a situation like that? It really took an enormous amount of guts and courage.

Thinking back to that day, that one act of kindness from a complete stranger touched me in a very deep and profound way. It has continued to stick with me after all of these years!

In the midst of searching for the answers to all of my pressing questions, I was faced with the events surrounding my father's funeral.

On the first day of his viewing, there was an enormous crowd in attendance. Just like when my mother had been put to rest, the funeral home was packed. In fact, the crowd was so big that it not only filled two main rooms but even exceeded all of the extra seating in the overflow area.

As I stood there in the middle of the crowds of people, I still felt numb and disconnected. People surrounded me, saying all kinds of things to express their condolences, but all I could see was their lips moving. I was too deep in my own grief and in my own thoughts to hear their words spoken out loud.

At the same time, I felt extremely protective over my dad. I wondered what everyone was really thinking as they came to pay their respects. If I took the time to listen, I could hear a lot of nice words, but I was well-acquainted with candy-coated talk.

What were the people really thinking?

I thought to myself, "Yes, my dad had taken his own life. Did everyone think he was weak-minded? Or did they think he took the easy way out? Did they think he was selfish or a coward to leave behind his four kids and his six grandchildren?"

I had to set the record straight! It was up to me to uphold my dad's honor and protect his legacy.

I found my legs in sudden motion, taking me all the way to the front of the joined rooms where I stood before my dad's casket. As if in a deep fog, I faced the people and found all eyes on me.

The room had turned completely silent. It was so quiet that anyone could have heard a pin drop. I had been quiet all day, but now, I opened my mouth and spoke. It was an untimely eulogy, completely unplanned and definitely not prewritten.

As I spoke from the deepest place in my heart, I talked about my dad's character, his undeniable love for my mother, his love for his children, and his life of devotion to God. I reminded everyone about who my dad truly was and how he had blessed each and every person present at some point or another in their lives. I told them that my dad was not weak-minded or selfish, but that the actions he displayed throughout his life were a true megaphone of hope and love—a powerful message for us all as we watched him live it out.

As I finished my speech, a line began to form in front of me. Men and women, including fathers and mothers, stood before me with tears flowing down their faces, just aching to talk to me, hug me, kiss me on my cheek, and tell me how much my words meant to them.

"I can only hope and pray that when my time comes, that my son or daughter has the boldness to speak like you did—and that they would say the same thing about me!" I heard this from multiple parents.

They knew, after all, that my father and I were best friends, so they all felt that they had just witnessed something extraordinary.

The final day of my dad's funeral arrived. It was time for me to fulfill the promise that I had made to my father as he lay in that cold hospital bed. I was devoted to making sure that he was laid to rest next to my mother—his wife and the love of his life.

That morning, while I was preparing for the day, I realized deep down inside that it was the very last time that I would ever see my dad. To be honest, I wasn't at all ready to say goodbye to him. I already missed him so much.

As soon as I entered the funeral home, I quickly dashed into the room where my dad was lying. I couldn't wait to be close to him. I had to make sure he was sleeping peacefully and that everything was all right. I had to fulfill my duty as a faithful son who always protected his family.

As I ran toward my dad's casket, the entire weight of my grief and agony suddenly struck me with full force. My legs gave out on me, and I collapsed onto the floor. Fortunately, I was already at the front of the room, so I landed on my knees—right onto the kneeler before my dad's casket.

For the past week, I had felt like the proverbial boy with his finger stuck in the dam, holding back the ocean so it would not wash away the entire village while pretending to be strong for others. I couldn't hold back the tumultuous seas any longer.

Falling forward, I began to cry, yet this was no ordinary cry. This hurt on the deepest level—it felt as if every bone in my body was breaking one after the other, from the top of my head down to the soles of my feet. My heart felt like it was being stabbed many times over and over.

I began to moan and wail from the deepest place in my soul—a most hideous and pathetic sound that I had absolutely no control over. I could no longer hold it together or stop it. The horrible noise just kept coming out of me and even grew louder. My body was shaking and trembling as I continued to groan in the deepest of agony.

Reality had finally hit me—it was all over! My dad—my best friend, MY HERO—was gone. In fact, both of my parents were gone. I was only twenty-five and now an orphan—alone without parents and left without answers.

When I finally recovered from my meltdown, I weakly pulled myself together. It was time to take my father to his final resting place. I had the honor of carrying my father out to the hearse, accompanying him to the cemetery, and bringing him to the place where he would rest in peace.

Despite the deep grief that was crushing me, I felt a sense of relief. This was my last great show of strength, honor, and integrity—a final salute to my father as he took his last ride to go join my mother, being laid to rest right beside her as he went to meet his true love once again in eternity. I had truly fulfilled my word to my dad and honored all of his last wishes.

It brought me a sense of pride, knowing that I did everything I could. I left the cemetery after the graveside ceremony, imagining the way that my parents would joyfully celebrate their reunion. I could envision them running to one another in laughter and delight, leaping into each other's arms after such a painful separation. They were together again at last—and now it would be forever.

As happy as I was to think about that sight, it was doubly hard on me. I missed my parents dreadfully and thought about them every day. I cried myself to sleep every night, longing to wake in the morning to hear their voices, just wanting to see them one last time.

Whoever said that time heals all wounds obviously never faced the kind of loss that I went through. The memories—both good and bad—were always there, heaping on more hurt and pain as I faced them in the cold stillness of the night and woke to yet another empty day.

Even now, these memories still haunt me. Just think—to experience such an upbringing only to have it end in such tragedy and be left with so many unanswered questions. It opened a senseless void in my heart that I thought could never be filled, which only served to send frightful shivers down my spine about what lay ahead in my future.

"What's next?"

"Where do I go from here?"

"Why did all of this happen?!"

That cross that I was carrying around with me day and night just had another major layer added to it. Even as I tried my best to bear the Cross of Deep

Regret, Grief, Misery, and now AGONY, I felt that the added weight was an enormous blow, making it nearly impossible to carry any longer.

Chapter 6

The Quest for Truth

I n the days ahead, I tried to put all of the pieces back together again, but I was deeply broken. I found myself without love—unable to love others and unable to love myself. I was empty inside, feeling lost, dazed, and confused with nowhere to run and nowhere to hide.

Nothing that I did seemed to be working. Something had to change, and something had to be done! I could no longer live this way.

Suicide suddenly became an option. The mere thought of it was almost inviting. After all, if my father couldn't make it through life, how could I?

Yet, I wasn't quite ready to give up on life. I just had to find the answers to the many questions that constantly swirled through my mind. So, I pressed on, living in misery but still searching for something to offer me comfort.

September 11, 2001, arrived—just two weeks and one day after my father's passing. I worked the third shift, so I came home early in the morning to find the phone ringing like crazy. I didn't pay it much attention as I just needed to get settled in after a long night. Plus, I honestly didn't feel like talking to anyone.

I headed to the kitchen and grabbed a beer from the fridge, opening it up and taking my first well-deserved swig of the day. It was what I did every morning after my shift, finding it a way to unwind before getting some sleep and then heading back to work by early afternoon.

Returning to the living room, I sat down and flicked on the TV, surprised to see breaking news taking place before my very eyes.

"Attacks on American Soil!" the headline blared.

Pictures came rolling in from New York, Pennsylvania, and Virginia as the story began to come together. Four commercial airlines en route to various destinations had been hijacked by suicide bombers who managed to gain control of the cockpits and fly the planes directly to their intended targets—the Pentagon and the World Trade Center, both North and South towers. As for the fourth plane, it crashed in a field in Pennsylvania somewhere since the passengers fought back to save the aircraft.

The world was in complete and utter chaos! America had been attacked!

Stunned by the news, I grabbed my phone to call my dad. I wanted to see if he was watching all of this unfold as well. I wanted to hear his thoughts and gain some wisdom and understanding from him.

As my dad's phone kept ringing and ringing, it suddenly hit me.

"My dad is gone. My dad isn't going to answer the phone because he's no longer with me."

I couldn't believe it! I mentally kicked myself in the most savage way possible, feeling anger and frustration mixing with the grief and pain that I had already been facing in my dad's absence.

"What am I thinking? Why haven't I realized that he's gone—never to return?

I had no answer to these questions, except to admit from a deep place within my wounded heart that I needed my dad. Instead of having him to turn to, however, I came to the harsh reality that I was completely on my own and had no one to go to in time of need.

As I continued to gaze at the TV, I watched the terror on the faces of the people at Ground Zero. My heart began to break, and I began to cry. It wasn't one of those hard cries—you know, the ones where you have to catch your breath. No, instead, these tears were gentle as they streamed down my face.

I began to feel the terror, the fear, the heartache, and the loss that I imagined taking place in these people's hearts and minds. I watched the images of the firefighters who were covered in soot—fighting the fires, recovering the lost, and saving those who were still alive and needed to be rescued. It was devastating to watch.

I thought to myself, "My God, my God! Where are You??!!! How could You let this happen?? Who would do such a thing?? And why??"

I felt deep compassion for these people as I heard about the loss of life, including men, women, and even children. The number of lost souls kept rising—projected to be in the thousands. I thought about the family members left behind and how they, too, would have to suffer great loss, just like me. I felt helpless. There was nothing I could do!

That last thought alone was the one that truly broke my heart. As I heard about the brave men and women running into harm's way to save others, I resonated with their actions. I, too, was filled with genuine compassion for others and was willing to do whatever it took to help others in time of need.

Having a servant's heart for others was always a huge part of who I am, first taught to me by my parents as I watched them in action. That love and compassion was then solidified when I saw the effects it had on the hearts of the recipients. Lives were truly changed when people were touched by just one act of simple generosity and kindness.

In the days ahead, life only seemed to be getting harder on me. I visited my parents' gravesite almost every day. I still remember the feeling I had when I was there. Most of all, it was lonely. When I tried to talk to my parents, I felt like I was just speaking into the air. Although their bodies were lying beneath my feet, I knew they weren't really there.

My heart was beginning to harden. I wanted answers and I wanted them now! How could this happen to me and my family? All of us served the Lord—feeding the homeless, visiting the widows and orphans, and dedicating our home to be a safe haven and sanctuary of peace for all who needed help.

Why had all of that been suddenly taken away— not only from me but from all those who sought refuge from the solitude they were facing? Who else would be there for them now that the kindness shown through my parents' lives had been unexpectedly torn away?

Better yet, who was this loving God I had come to know and love through the life of my parents? Why had He forsaken me?

Why didn't He save my parents by stretching forth His arm to heal my mother or sending down an angel to stop the bullet that struck my father?

Why did He allow me to sign my father out of the mental ward the night before, knowing that he was only going to kill himself the following day? Perhaps if my dad had stayed where he was at then he'd still be alive today.

What about the last conversation I had with my mom, not knowing at the time that my last words to her would be spoken out of such hurt and anger?

Why had both of these situations gone down the way they did, forcing upon me the Cross of Deep Regret that I now had to bear? After all, I chose to show great disrespect to my mother, which left me ashamed. Then, I was the one who signed the release paperwork for my dad and brought him home. He was placed under my care and supervision!

And furthermore, what about that psychic who predicted my dad's untimely demise?!

Why wouldn't God at least talk to me or show me something to let me know that He was there and truly understood what I was going through?

Maybe what I had done was enough for Him to turn His back on me. After all, I deserved this misery. I began to believe that it was all my fault.

I had grown up to believe that He was a good God—all the time—and that He would never leave me or forsake me. He was ever so present in time of need, and He was loving and forgiving.

Yet, when I needed God the most, why was He silent? Was He even there, or did He even care? Worst of all, was He even real?

I was determined to find out the Truth about this God that I still claimed to love but was now quickly losing faith in. In fact, my faith had been shaken to its very core by these tragic events. I was now faced with many doubts and wondered if He was just some myth that my parents believed in to help them get through life.

I decided to go see one of my parents' friends who just so happened to be a pastor and ask him a couple of questions. He knew my parents well and was a good friend of the family. I liked this man, I trusted his thoughts, and I loved to watch him preach.

When I arrived at his office building and knocked on his private door, the man invited me in.

"How are you doing?" he immediately asked me, already knowing what I was going through.

I replied that I was having a very hard time but that I would eventually get through everything.

He said, "That's to be expected—your parents were great people." Then he invited me to sit down and faced me from behind his desk. "What can I do for you?"

I told him that I was there because I had a couple of questions for him.

He nodded and replied, "Sure, go ahead and ask."

Looking at him straight in the eyes, I asked him plainly, "Where do you think my parents are?"

You see, since the time I was growing up, I knew that there were only two possible places for people to end up when they died—either Heaven or Hell. I was pretty sure I knew where my mom was, but I had certain doubts about my dad. We had been taught that suicide was a one-way ticket to Hell, no questions asked. If a person took their own life, they were forever damned.

The pastor looked at me compassionately and said, "Donnie, your mother was a God-fearing woman. It was a great loss to the faith the day she died." He concluded by saying, "Rest easy, Son— your mother is with the Lord in Heaven."

I already had felt the same way about my mom, so that's not really why I had come. I pressed him further. "Where's my father?"

He gazed at me for a moment and then quietly answered, "Although your father was a great man and a megaphone of love and hope to all who knew him, your father's decision to take his own life landed him in Hell. The Bible is clear on this, as it says, 'If any man should take his own life, he has condemned himself to the Lake of Fire.' I'm sorry that I have to be the one to tell you this, Donnie."

I had been staring at the pastor as he spoke, and then I immediately rose. "Thank you for your time," I said rigidly, heading for the door.

As I got back into my truck, I slammed the door hard, red-hot fury coursing through me. How could he say that about my dad? They had been friends! Plus, my dad faithfully paid his tithes to his church house. How dare this man tell me that my father was not only burning in Hell but suffering in the Lake of Fire!!!

That was it! I turned the key in the ignition and spun out of the drive, headed for home. Along the way, I stopped at every bookstore I saw and grabbed every version of the Bible I could find.

"If any man should take his own life, he has condemned himself to the Lake of Fire" indeed! I had to see this verse for myself! I could no longer accept another man's word as truth unless I saw it on my own.

Once I got home, I stacked all of the Bibles in a tall pile on the coffee table beside my favorite reclining chair and got to work. I searched and searched through every version I had, combing through the Old Testament and New Testament for those fateful words.

I even went to the library to look at older versions that dated as far back as 1611 and 1539, looking for a verse that simply wasn't there.

As my stack of Bibles dwindled, I began to have second thoughts. Perhaps I had overlooked the verse during the countless hours I had spent searching. But hold on a second—this kind of research wasn't anything new to me. I was used to diving into critical topics time and time again. If my mother was still here, she would be the first to say that my research was meticulous!

Although I knew in my heart that I was right and that this so-called verse never existed, I gave the pastor the benefit of the doubt. I went back to see him so I could ask him to show me exactly where the verse was located. Of course, I had my trusty stack of Bibles with me.

Walking into his office, I laid the first book on his desk, asking him, "Can you show me where that verse is about my dad being in the Lake of Fire?"

The pastor looked up at me, blinking owlishly. "Uhm, you're not going to find that verse in the Bible, Donnie," he began to say.

"Okay," I said, cutting him off. "Here's a different Bible! Can you show it to me in this one?"

"No," the pastor replied.

"Okay, here's another version! How about this one?"

"No," he said patiently. "You won't find it in that one either."

I went through my whole stack of Bibles to hear him say that about every last one! Finally, all of the books were sprawled out across his desk. I stood there, staring down at him, awaiting an explanation.

"You see," the man offered, putting on his most pastoral tone, "it's not actually a God-spoken verse. It's more of—well, a doctrinal belief that is used to keep people from committing suicide."

Feeling my face turn hot in anger, I replied, "Oh! So, now you're lying to the people! By your own admission, you put words in God's mouth, adding to the Word of God! So, this is just a doctrine of man that has become a belief, but it is actually far from the truth!"

The pastor moved a bit uncomfortably in his chair and then shrugged, extending his hands toward me in a plea. "Well, I believe that God doesn't really mind. The intentions are good anyway and used to save lives."

"You care about saving lives?" I demanded, grabbing one of the Bibles off of the desk and quickly flipping over to Deuteronomy 4:2. "Well, hear this!"

I then read him a verse, "Ye shall not add unto the word which I command you, neither shall ye diminish ought from it, that ye may keep the commandments of the LORD your God which I command you!"

The man's jaw dropped as he continued to listen to me speak.

"How about saving your own life?! Think of the danger that you put your soul in!" I went on, unabated. "Lying on God and lying to the people who entrust themselves to you for their spiritual growth and well-being! You would have done better to just tell me that you don't know exactly where my dad is and leave that decision up to God. He alone is both Judge and jury!"

With that, I stacked up all my Bibles and walked out of that man's office, never to return. I distinctly felt betrayed and hurt by the so-called church that I once called home.

At the same time, I knew in my heart that I never was a religious person—nor am I today. I had seen what religion does to people, bringing forth division with this denomination versus that denomination, each governed by their own set of what they call by-laws.

I also knew that the so-called church was the biggest cause of atheism in the modern world, and I wanted no part in it. I was taught that we were all called to live in peace and unity, not separated by religious beliefs and doctrinal disbeliefs.

As a matter of fact, I was certain that the only religious thing I would ever be devoted to was known quite simply as pure and undefiled religion before God the Father—to visit the fatherless and widows in their affliction and to keep oneself unspotted from the world.

You see, living a life of faith to me was all about relationships, not just with God but also with others. Faith wasn't about doctrinal beliefs or the religious system that people call the church—it was about living and dwelling among other people with compassion, humility, and kindness. It included building relationships together, learning from one another, and growing through hardships one step at a time.

I thought about all of the essential points that went along with my idea of relationships—receiving encouragement from those who already went through tough spots in life and giving encouragement to those who hadn't; doing unto others as I would have done unto myself; finding understanding in the middle of great confusion and conflict; and loving my enemies. Then there was the most important of all—to love the Lord my God with all my heart, mind, and soul. I knew that true life was found on the outside of the walls of what these people called a church, not tucked away within them.

Yet, all of this no longer mattered to me. Life no longer existed as I knew it. Instead, it seemed like a quickly-fading blur—dark, cold, and empty. I saw no light at the end of this tunnel.

I just wanted to be alone. The only place I could think of going was to my parents' cemetery. After all, it was a balmy summer day—the sun was shining, it was ninety degrees, and there was a gentle breeze coming from the west. It was the perfect day for a beautiful drive in the countryside.

So, I stacked up the Bibles into the passenger seat of my truck and headed north to the cemetery. As I got closer, I stopped at a nearby field that my mother used to love due to the wildflowers that grew there. She especially loved daisies.

I picked a nice assortment of different flowers that I knew my mom would love and my dad would appreciate before completing my drive. Walking up to the place where their bodies now rested, I placed the flowers into the potter attached to their headstone and sat down to think.

Many memories from my youth came flashing through my mind. It was as if I was actually reliving those moments. I could see the smiles on my parents' faces, hearing their laughter as they talked together, and recognizing their voices as they called me. I pictured our lives together as a family, feeling the love and the joy that we shared.

Then, out of nowhere, I pictured my mother standing in the bathroom and looking into the mirror as she got ready for her doctor's appointment on that fateful day. As she fell to the ground, blood began coming out of her ears, nose, and mouth due to the brain aneurysm.

I heard her calling, "Donnie!" She was calling for ME to come help her, but I wasn't there.

Then, off in the distance, I heard the striking sound of a gunshot being fired. As the noise echoed through the air, I heard my dad's voice.

"Donnie!" he said. "I'm sorry, Son. Will you ever forgive me for leaving you?"

I quickly snapped out of that place in my mind. Anger began to course through me. I stood up, planting my feet firmly on the ground as if I was preparing for a fight.

Looking up at the sky, I pointed my finger accusingly in God's direction and yelled at Him. "YOU DID THIS!! YOU TOOK MY PARENTS AWAY FROM ME!! YOU DIDN'T EVEN LET ME SAY GOODBYE!!

"YOU CALL YOURSELF A LOVING GOD?!! WELL, HEAR THIS—I WILL NEVER SERVE YOU!! DO YOU HEAR ME?!! I WILL *NEVER* SERVE YOU!!"

At that moment, a threatening black cloud—and I mean BLACK—appeared over my head. A lightning bolt came crackling out of the sky, striking the ground about three feet from where I stood.

This scared the living daylights out of me! My fury now turned into terror, I immediately ran to take cover in my truck. I hopped in, slammed the door, turned the key in the ignition, and flew out of the cemetery as fast as I could.

When I looked into my rear view mirror, I noticed that as quickly as that black cloud had rolled in, it had instantly dissipated.

Still shaking in fear, I immediately cried out over and over, "I'm sorry, God! I'm sorry, God!" I was panicking, hoping that my apology would calm Him down.

At the same time, I wasn't truly sorry. I was still angry, upset, and mad at God. Even if He didn't directly cause all of the tragedy in my life, He easily could have prevented everything from happening. After all, He was God, right?

Yet, He didn't stop anything, and that's all I needed to know. My relationship with Him was now severed forever—or so I thought.

As I drove home, I didn't know what to expect, but the greatest sadness I had ever felt came over me. In fact, I felt deep remorse as I thought over the one-way conversation I just had with God. There was nothing more I could do. The words had already been spoken and the damage had been done.

What was to become of me now? While that answer was being weighed in the balance, I truly felt that I couldn't care less. I had given up on hope, making the Cross that I had been carrying for years become even heavier—now weighed down with the additional burdens of Disappointment and Remorse.

To be honest, I always was my own worst critic. The disappointment I was feeling didn't have anything to do with anyone else—I was simply disappointed in myself for being so weak-minded and feeling like a failure. Where I had once been strong in heart, mind, body, and soul, there was a vast emptiness.

If one would have taken a close look on the inside of me at that time to see what was really taking place, they would have seen a man who no longer had one ounce of strength, one shred of hope, or one bit of love to give to anyone— including himself. Instead, this man was now lying flat on his face in disgust at who he had become.

This nightmare was now my reality.

Chapter 7

The Battle of Good Versus Evil

Three years had passed, and I was now twenty-eight. Although I felt like I had given up on hope, I still had some fight left in me. I hadn't completely given up on love. I had to see for myself what lay ahead of me so I could find out if I would even be able to navigate through this life after enduring such tragedy.

I knew it wasn't going to be easy, and that I would have to face it like a man. I figured, after all that I had been through, what else could go wrong? I still hadn't received answers to any of the questions I had already asked and found myself in a total state of confusion.

Meanwhile, everything that could go wrong did go wrong. I was still self-medicating and growing more depressed by the day. I had gone through a divorce and was battling for visitation, now dealing with my family being broken apart as I rarely saw my two children. Long-term relationships I once had were severed. Life was spinning out of my control, and there was nothing I could do to stop it.

Yet, once again, on the outside, I appeared to be strong. I appeared to have it all together.

My friends even made comments, saying, "If I went through what you did, I don't honestly know how I'd be handling it!"

In their minds, they saw a strength in me that they could only hope to possess if the bottom in life ever fell out from under them.

Meanwhile, I was thinking, "If they only knew the deep, dark internal conflict I am dealing with, they wouldn't be thinking about me like this!"

After all, I was just a man—and a broken one at that.

Thinking back to my childhood, I grew up to believe that there were two powers in this world and that One was greater than the other. There was God, and there was Satan.

I heard and read about Heaven and Hell—how Heaven was so beautiful, having streets of transparent gold and rivers of milk and honey. It was a place where all tears were washed away—no more pain, no more sorrow, and no more suffering. Heaven was also filled with many mansions—a Kingdom filled with unspeakable joy, amazing grace, everlasting mercy, and all-encompassing love. I even dreamed about Heaven.

I also heard and read about Hell—a place of eternal fire, constant torment, and weeping and gnashing of teeth! It was a place where the worm never dies! I read about the Lake of Fire that burns with brimstone—a second death that brought forth everlasting punishment, a most wretched place filled with disgrace and shame, a place where each individual soul burned constantly, consumed in fire and brimstone for eternity!

I knew the battle of good versus evil, the fight for one's soul, was real—and it was taking place right on my doorstep. What I was dealing with couldn't be explained any other way. Satan had come in like a thief in the night to rob, destroy, and kill me. He had already robbed me of my family, he was in the midst of destroying me, and all he had left to do was take my life.

It was one attack right after the other—no option to breathe, no option for a two-minute time out—and just a constant barrage of physical, emotional, and mental attacks aimed at taking me out.

I was wounded and perplexed, and I felt abandoned. Every ounce of fight and courage left in me was now gone. This was no nightmare—I was faced with its cold, hard reality day in and day out. I wanted the pain to go away; I wanted the hurt to end.

I also didn't want to hurt anyone else emotionally, since I had heard that hurt people hurt people! I knew that my children had already been caught up in a situation that wasn't at all their fault, and I love my children like any good parent does. I didn't want to bring unneeded hurt to their innocent and precious lives, and I felt that they'd be better off without me.

So, I made a call and picked up an eight-ball of coke and a twelve-pack of beer. I was over life at this point and was going to end mine. My plan was simple—drink a few beers and dive headfirst with my nose and mouth into the mountain of coke I had just bought. I thought to myself that I would overdose and die.

It sounded terrible and selfish to me, but I couldn't take it anymore. I was without love and without hope, and I hated both my life and the pain and hurt associated with it. I had no idea what life was for. All I knew was that it was no longer for me—I wanted no part of it.

I drank a couple of beers and snorted a couple of lines, thinking, "Well, this is it—no one's here to stop me, and nobody's gonna save me."

Then I got up to rinse my nose clean from the previous lines I had done. The time had come—I was now in the final minutes of my life.

As I stood before the bathroom sink, I remember looking into the mirror at myself for one last time. I couldn't stand looking at myself! It was like looking into a face that I no longer recognized. I had become like the shell of a man I once saw in my father after my mother had passed away.

Just then, I heard a voice say, "Whatcha waiting for? No one is coming to save you. No one cares about you! Finish this, and let's be on our way. You're better off dead than alive."

I could see the evil spirit in the mirror. His face was black and that of a bull with horns, his eyes were black with red pupils, fire and smoke plumed from his nostrils when he spoke, and his body was that of a man who was a bodybuilder.

His voice was subtle, and he seemed irritated and in a rush. I sensed that he had this conversation with many others before me, and this was just another assignment he was on. He was demonic, and I knew that I didn't want to go wherever he thought he was going to take me.

I began to cry as I headed to the couch to take my last breath, knowing that I was going to fill it with cocaine—a most deadly poison. As I sat in position with tears streaming down my face, I called out for Jesus!

I called His name three times, "JESUS! JESUS! JESUS!"

I had always known in my heart that His Name was the Name above all names and that in the Name of Jesus, every demon must flee.

As I cried out, Jesus showed up! His radiance filled the living room, and His majestic glory consumed my entire apartment.

He spoke and said, "I am here, my son! Tell me what's wrong."

I felt like He had picked me up and coddled me like I was a newborn baby.

I said, "Oh, Jesus, my heart is broken! I'm no longer able to love others, let alone myself. My heart is broken—fix it, Jesus, fix it!"

At that moment, I felt His hand go into my chest as He began to stitch my heart back together, piece by piece.

As He did so, I told Him how I signed my father out of the hospital, only to find out that my dad would later take his own life. I told Him how I cussed my mother out the night before she passed away, and how ashamed I was. I told Him how my kids no longer had a full-time father. I told Him all about the guilt I was carrying and all about the pain and hurt it caused me.

Jesus said to me, "My son, you're carrying a cross that wasn't meant for you to carry. Give it to me."

I instantly replied, "Take it, Jesus, take it!"

At that moment, I felt a heavy weight—an enormous burden—being lifted off of my chest and shoulders. That cross I once carried, both day and night, was now gone.

My heart was made new! The depression and all that was associated with my hurt and pain was gone! I felt a love I never knew, a safety and security that was impenetrable!

Meanwhile, that demon that had spoken to me had vanished, and it was just Jesus and me.

That night, I told Him everything. I poured my heart out to Him as I wept and wept.

He said to me, "Rest now, my son."

I asked Jesus not to leave me. I told Him how much I needed Him, how much I missed Him, and how much I loved Him. I told Him how sorry I was for doubting Him and how sorry I was for telling Him that I would never serve Him.

Jesus replied, "You are forgiven, and I have always loved you with an everlasting love. I have never left you and will never forsake you. You are My child, and I am your Father. Rest now, for we have much to talk about."

As I slept, I felt a warmth and peace that flowed throughout my entire body. I now heard the new rhythm of my heart that was no longer broken. I knew wholeheartedly that everything was going to be okay!

When I awoke the next morning, His presence engulfed me and His love surrounded me. I felt like a new man! My life had been spared, and there was this peace that surpassed all understanding surrounding me with an unspeakable joy beaming within me that had not been there just twenty-four hours ago.

I knew that the storm wasn't over and that I had many things to face, but I no longer had to face it alone. My confidence, my hope, and my faith in Him had been restored! My weakness was now turned to strength, and I now had the courage to fight this battle, knowing that He, Jesus, was by my side!

Chapter 8

A Passion is Born

During this time in my life, the Lord was constantly talking to me as He continued to work on my heart. I began to realize that He had always been speaking to me through every step of my journey, but I had somehow tuned Him out.

It amazed me to know that He was with me, standing right beside me and just waiting for me to ask Him for His help! The Lord is not one to take away anyone's free will, as He will not impose Himself on anyone unless He's invited. I realized that even though I was talking to Him throughout my struggles, I hadn't actually asked Him for His help until the day He spared my life. I actually had been too busy blaming Him for everything that had happened.

As I was reading my Bible, I came across a passage that said, "He that has ears to hear, let them hear." In another place, it read, "But blessed are your eyes, for they see, and your ears, for they hear."

It spoke volumes to me since I knew that the Lord was instructing me and speaking a blessing into and over my life. All I had to do was just dare to believe that what He said was true. Why wouldn't I now? I had just encountered Him, and it blessed my heart. I was no longer self-medicating, and the thoughts of suicide were gone.

I even thought to myself, "What in the world was I thinking?!!"

As I began to ponder all of the things that had taken place in my life, it became apparent to me that God did, in fact, have a calling for me. What my mother and father and all of those people had said to me as a child was true.

I still didn't know what His plan and purpose was for me, but I began to see life in a different light, and I began to experience things in different ways. I knew that nothing ever happens by coincidence and that everything in life happens for a reason. My perspective had now become altogether different.

I began reflecting on my past, remembering how I had grown up experiencing life and death at a very early age. I had heard stories of both good and evil from those who sought refuge in the companionship of my parents. I had heard about their trials and tribulations. I had seen how life was unpredictable and came with its many challenges.

It was tragic to hear those people cry and ask the question, "Why is this happening to me?"

I watched as their hearts broke and tears fell from their eyes, but I also saw the gentle and heartfelt compassion that my parents gave to each and every person.

I heard their prayers as they sought answers that they knew only the Lord could give. I also watched as their prayers were being answered! I saw those people who had once been broken and without hope come back to life, rejoicing in the Lord as they became stronger after the fact than before. I was now being enlightened and awakened to a universe that had always been two worlds within one—a carnal world filled with nature and people, and a heavenly realm consisting of spiritual matters and beings.

Even as a child, I saw that there was a need, a cry for help, and I realized the great importance and impact my parents had in the personal lives of so many others.

I now had that same desire and a willingness to reach as many as I could in any way that I could. I now had a story! There was now a light at the end of my tunnel which would guide me on the rest of my journey.

As I continued to flip through the pages of my Bible, I came across a letter written to me by my mom. It was dated December 2, 1997, the very day she had passed away.

I had never seen this letter before! It was like it had been gently tucked away within the many pages of the Book. I knew that this Bible was my last gift from her as she bought it to give to me that Christmas.

The letter said,

"Donnie,

You are my son and I love you and I'm so proud of you. If you look Deeply into your Heart, you will see that I have always been here. May the Peace of God

Be Richly in Your Soul and May His Love Surround You! I love you, son, and Jesus does, too. For where your treasure is, there will your heart be also.

Love,

Mom and Dad"

Tears began to stream down my face, as I knew that she had written it the same morning before her death, just after our conversation and argument the prior night. She had already forgiven me and wanted me to know how deep her love for me truly was!

I remember saying in a gentle voice, almost in a whisper, "Oh, Mom, I am so sorry for what I said to you! Just know that I love you, too, and miss you very much. Thank you for placing me in the hands of God."

It brought such a healing to my heart, knowing that I had been forgiven and that my mom held no animosity in her heart toward me. While there was still sadness over our last encounter, there was also gladness.

That experience taught me a very important life lesson—To always be mindful of what we say to others because our words hold weight and may sometimes cause regret, especially in knowing that we are not promised tomorrow and are unaware of what tomorrow may bring.

Once again, the Lord was answering my prayers one minute at a time, one step at a time, and one day at a time. He truly is the Repairer of the Breech and the Restorer of the Paths we dwell in!

As you can see, not only was I maturing as a man, but more importantly, I was maturing spiritually and healing emotionally. Where I once had confusion, I now had clarity. Where I once had conflict, I now had peace.

My sorrow turned to happiness and my misery turned to joy! I now had a new love for life and for others. The same feelings I had as a small child and a young boy were now being restored, and that was something that I had always hoped for. I now had a purpose!

I understood that just because Jesus saved my life that day, it didn't mean that my life was now going to be a bed of roses or that it would be made perfect here on earth.

In fact, it was just the opposite, as He tells us, "In this world, you will have trials and you will have tribulations, but be of good cheer! Take heart!!! For I, Jesus, have overcome the world!"

And, "Knowing that He is before all things and in Him all things hold together!!"

At this point, even my prayer life had changed. Instead of praying once a day, I was now praying morning, noon, and night while also talking to Him throughout my day.

At night, before I went to bed, I always knelt next to it while I prayed. My prayers even began to change. I began to pray according to His will, and not my will be done.

I prayed for the widows, that they, too, would find companionship, having someone to care for again.

I prayed for the orphans who were without a home and family and had nothing to eat, that they, too, would find a family who truly loved and cared for them and would never again have to go without a hot meal.

I prayed for the homeless, poor, and needy, that the Lord would supply all of their needs according to His riches and glory.

I prayed for my children, that one day if trouble should ever come their way they would know exactly who to turn to. I prayed that the Lord would protect them and keep them from all evil and that they, too, would walk with the Lord all the days of their lives.

I prayed against generational curses like suicide, addictions, guilt, and depression.

I prayed for those who were suffering from sicknesses and various types of cancers.

I prayed that Jesus would share His heart with me so that I could love others as He does.

I even prayed for my enemies.

Most importantly, I prayed for YOU.

I wasn't just praying for those here in America. I was also praying for all those across the world— every tribe, every nation, and every tongue. After all, aren't we all created in His image and likeness? Aren't we all called to pray one for another?

I was being renewed, and I was being transformed. It felt like I had died to my old self and had been reborn again. I watched the door to my old life begin to close while a new door set upon a different path was being opened and revealed.

I began to experience visions and dreams. Allow me to share with you the story of the first vision that He showed me.

One evening, I was getting ready for a Bible study and the Lord spoke to me.

He said, "I have seen you many times."

I quickly responded, "Of course You have! You knew me before You placed me in my mother's womb."

The Lord spoke again and said, "No, I have seen you many times."

This time, His voice was stern, and I knew that He was trying to tell me something. So, I decided not to immediately respond until I could seek a better answer.

After my Bible study, I came home. I was tired and it was late, but I always prayed before I went to sleep, kneeling in front of my bed each and every night.

The next day came and all I could think about was my conversation with the Lord from the previous evening. I had already been going through the Scriptures, looking for a better response.

I thought, "For sure, I have found one!" So, I said, "Okay, Lord, here's where You have seen me many times," and quoted Him yet another Scripture.

His reply was louder and more stern than the last, as he said, "NO!! I have seen you many times."

At this point, I didn't know what to think! At best, I was baffled.

So, I said, "Lord, whatever do You mean? What are You trying to tell me?"

I received no response.

Day three arrived, and I still had no answer from the Lord. I was extremely curious about what He meant by saying that He had seen me many times.

That night, as I knelt before my bed to pray, I began to ask Him, "What did You mean by telling me, 'I have seen you many times'?"

As I was praying in this manner, He spoke to me and said, "Open your eyes."

I did so, and I looked and saw, both to my left and to my right, as far as the eye could see, the multitude of saints on their knees praying in different languages before the very Throne of God! And I was somewhere in the midst of them!

I said to the Lord, "You mean to tell me that every time I pray, You see me, even in the midst of such a great multitude, and that I literally place myself before Your Throne in Your Throne Room?!!"

He replied, "This is where I have seen you many times!"

In that moment, I felt a shrinking feeling come over me as I asked, "Who am I, Lord, that You are ever so mindful of me?"

The Lord responded, "You are My son, and I have loved you with an everlasting love."

The magnitude of His power, the love of His heart, and His concern for all the things that He created both big and small just floored me!

The multitude of saints praying as their petitions were being heard and answered was more than the human mind could understand. It was much bigger than life—it was eternal, and I had seen it with my very own eyes. I knew from that moment on, my life was never going to be the same again.

Some of you may be thinking that I should have already known that my life would never be the same again, especially after my encounter with Jesus. But we as humans tend to cast doubt first and question the things we see, hear, and feel later.

We begin to ask ourselves, "Did I just really hear that?" and "Why am I feeling this way?" or "Did I actually just see that happen?"

This is a very normal reaction to have when we ourselves cannot explain the unknown, let alone the supernatural. Trust me, I too have asked these questions many times.

While others of you may be asking yourselves, "Who is this person?"

To you, I answer and say, "I'm just a normal, ordinary human being, a person like you, a man who was once broken and who is now being made whole again. I am a man who just dared to believe that every word God spoke through His word is true!"

Chapter 9

Breakfast and a Cup of Coffee

Life was altogether changing for me. I met a girl, and we had a lot in common. She was outgoing and loved to laugh. She was quite the movie buff and used funny quotes and punchlines from her favorite films to make others laugh.

You could tell just by her charisma that she enjoyed being around others who made her laugh as well. She seemed to always have a smile on her face and had a genuine love for life, which was something I desperately needed in my life at that time. She had a love for poetry, was a writer of sorts, and was extremely talented when it came to her art.

We were really excited about one another. I remember thinking, though, that I would wait a couple of days to call her after our first date, not wanting to seem too eager or risk the chance of scaring her off.

To my surprise, she called me the very next morning to ask me if I would like to come see her and meet her parents. I guess when she got home, she was all excited and told her mom and dad all about me.

Of course, I said, "Yes!" and headed right over there. I was excited about her and curious to meet her parents while looking forward to getting to know more about her.

As I arrived, she was waiting for me on her front doorstep. I stepped out of my car, and she greeted me with a smile and a huge hug.

Then she said, "My mother is very excited to meet you, as she thinks she might already know who you are."

I kinda smirked and said, "Really?"

She said, "You'll see, c'mon!" Once again, she smiled and then grabbed my hand, pulling me toward her mom who was standing just a few feet away, looking out the front door at me.

As I entered the living room where her mother and father were, her mother looked at me and said, "Your parents wouldn't happen to be Donald and Theresa, would they?"

Of course, I replied, "Yes, ma'am, that's them."

She then said, "Omigosh, when my daughter told me your name, I just knew it! How are they doing?"

I told her that my parents had passed away and how it happened.

She was shocked and seemed extremely sad to hear the news since she and my mother were best friends in school but had lost touch with each other over the years. They shared a lot of memories together, and she shared some of those stories with me that I had never heard before.

She even told me that she was the one who introduced my father to my mother! She told me that my father was such a dreamer and that he always spoke of traveling and buying a big house one day.

At that, she just kinda chuckled and smiled, asking about the lifestyle they had lived.

I told her, "Well, my dad bought that big ole house, and he and my mom traveled all around the country during his vacations from work."

She smiled in amazement and said, "Good for them! Your mother was a very special person—as was your father!"

From that day on, her daughter and I were nearly inseparable. We ended up getting married and had a child—a beautiful baby girl with red hair and blue eyes, which was something my wife had always dreamed about and desired. She had even prayed specifically for red hair and blue eyes.

Life was great. We had our moments, of course, just like every other couple does. Yet, at the end of the day, we knew that neither one of us was ever going to leave the other—or so we thought.

I began working out of town, about two hours away. It was easier for me to stay close to my job and come home on the weekends. It was hard on us to be apart and even tougher on the baby, but we needed the money. What else could we do? Jobs were hard to come by, especially ones that paid over minimum wage. Plus, I just started this job. Still, it was very hard on me, and I missed them both, especially since our daughter was just a newborn.

A few months went by and Easter was approaching, so we made a plan for her to come, pick me up, and take me home for the weekend. We wanted to celebrate as a family.

So, she and the baby came and picked me up. We were excited to see each other and had a lot to talk about on the two-hour drive home.

As we were just getting into town, about twenty minutes from where we lived, we were hit by a drunk driver who was also high on cocaine. T-boned, to be exact, as he drove straight into the driver's side of the car, sending our vehicle airborne and flipping it multiple times through the air.

At that moment, I felt the hand of God consume the interior of that car. There's no other way for me to explain it.

When our car came crashing down, it landed upside down with the wheels in the air. My wife and I were knocked unconscious—she was driving, I was in the passenger seat, and our beautiful baby girl was strapped in her car seat as we were all left hanging upside down.

I quickly came to, as gasoline began pouring out all over the vehicle—and us. I glanced over to see my wife, almost lifeless. I looked into the back seat to check on my daughter, and as I did, I saw two hands reaching in from the outside of the car to pull her out, as every window was now shattered.

I unbuckled myself and slid out of the car, running around to the driver's side to pull my wife from the wreck. I couldn't free her since her seat belt was locked and stuck.

Now on my knees, I screamed for help in fear that the car was going to catch fire. At the same time, I was asking, "Where is my daughter?" in a panic.

Immediately, I heard the voice of a woman tell me that my daughter was fine, just as a man simultaneously ran over to hand me a knife to cut my wife loose. The man and I both slid my wife out of the car and moved her to safety. The car caught fire just seconds later.

My wife was still unconscious. I knew she had taken the brunt of the impact and was seriously injured. My daughter, however, escaped without any injuries. A small crowd formed around us, standing nearby, and looking on with shocked faces.

We were transported by ambulance to two separate hospitals—my daughter and I went to one while my wife went to another that was known for its specialty in trauma care. The hospitals were about a half-hour away from each other.

When my daughter and I got to the hospital, she was taken to one room, and I was taken to another that was right next door and had a glass window separating us. I could see my daughter as the nurses and doctors carefully checked her over. Not one hair on her head was harmed, and she was just fine!

I, however, had suffered a concussion, multiple contusions, and fourteen broken ribs. The staff in the ER planned to do x-rays on me to check for internal bleeding.

While all this was going on, I wanted an update on my wife. I had to know how she was doing, and if she was even alive.

The staff called the hospital where she had been taken and requested an update. I learned through them that my wife was in critical condition and fighting for her life. At that point, I decided to check myself out of the hospital, declining any more medical treatment.

What else could I do? My wife and daughter needed me. Who was going to take care of them if I was laid up in the hospital? Who was going to take care of my daughter? Their needs were way more important to me than a couple of broken ribs, and I was going to see to it that I was there to fill their needs no matter what!

By that time, my uncle showed up at the hospital, saying that he had seen the accident on the news, and rushed right over. He asked me what I was doing and why I was signing myself out of the hospital. He told me that I was in no condition to walk and that I had to let the emergency staff do their job.

I told him that I had to get to my wife and that I had to take care of my daughter. Although I was in great pain myself, we left and headed to where my wife was.

At that hospital, I was greeted by her mother who told me that they weren't allowing any visitors. My wife was still in surgery—one of many to come. Her pelvic bone had been broken in three different places, her spleen had been severed, she lost the use of one of her kidneys, and she had bitten completely through her tongue. As if that wasn't enough, there was more—she was in a state of temporary paralysis, and she would now suffer partial complex seizures.

Her father was also there, but he didn't want to see me or talk to me, as it was now my fault that his baby girl was fighting for her life.

My wife was still alive, even though the road to recovery was going to be long and very hard. She spent many months in rehab, facing several life-altering surgeries both at the hospital and the nursing facility.

Meanwhile, I was taking care of our baby girl on my own while doing my best to heal. We were both preparing for my wife to finally come home.

She still could not walk, and the mobility in her arms and hands was only at twenty percent. She got a couple of staph infections, which required proper care—packing and unpacking her wounds with gauze and a saline solution three to four times a day. She was on a powerful antibiotic that was given to her through an IV and PICC line.

As the medical equipment was being delivered to our house, I was also being trained as her primary caregiver. My wife would require care twenty-four hours around the clock. My daughter and I were just finally glad to have her home.

The days ahead came with many difficult challenges as one could only imagine. Yet another trial had unexpectedly come into my life and the lives of my family.

I prayed continually over my wife's life and recovery. I thanked the Lord for His divine intervention, as everyone who was associated with the accident swore that we shouldn't be alive. They told us that we were walking and talking miracles!

The car itself looked like one of those aluminum cans that had been totally crushed. The mere sight of it told a completely different story with a very grim outcome than what actually had taken place.

I knew that this had to be an attack of the enemy in an attempt to take not only my life but my family's lives also. As I thought about the accident and remembered what I had felt as we were being violently tossed through the air, a verse came to me out of nowhere. It says. "When the enemy shall come in like a flood, the Spirit of the LORD shall lift up a standard against him!" Once again, the Lord had not only spared and saved my life but the lives of my wife and daughter as well.

As I thought about everything and realized that the enemy was back to using his same old tactics, I began to get angry. I knew that he's not a creator but rather an imitator with no new thoughts of his own, merely lurking like a roaming lion and seeking whomever he may devour.

The enemy was also trying to guilt me for the accident with the subtle mention of cocaine. As life and death flashed before my eyes once again, I had many things to wonder about.

For instance, I thought, "Who is this man who unexpectedly drove into our lives uninvited, almost killing the three of us, and being drunk and high— behind the wheel of his car while completely out of his mind?!"

I knew the battle for my life was real, and I knew Satan wasn't going to stop, but I also knew my first line of defense was prayer.

I figured that perhaps the enemy didn't get the memo, or maybe he did and just forgot. I figured it was time that I remind him that I wasn't the same young man he approached years before while seeking after my life in yet another attempt to destroy me.

No, not even in the least! I was now spiritually aware of who Satan was and what tactics he used. My eyes had been opened and enlightened, my life had been spared yet again, and I now had a purpose. I was now being loved by a Love so great that the enemy himself COULD NOT MOVE ME.

I was, in fact, a child of the Most High God and had always been. I was here to stand my ground and to fight, knowing what the enemy intended for evil against me that God was going to turn around and use for His Glory.

I began to pray, thinking about that man who hit us. I began to forgive him! I prayed over his life and that of his family. I prayed that one day, he too would find peace for his soul, turning away from his addictions and placing his eyes upon the Lord. Having never met this man, I felt that it was the right thing to do. As I finished praying, my anger was gone, and my peace had been restored!

The next step was physical therapy and rehabilitation for my wife, as she was home and we had already put a plan in place—one we made over the phone when she called from the nursing facility each and every day. I promised her that, together, we were going to conquer this challenge, and she would walk again. She couldn't agree more.

My wife knew that it wasn't going to be easy, but she had a tenacity about her—sheer determination and the will power to walk again, to play with her daughter again, and to overcome being bound to a wheelchair.

Every day, she fought harder than the last—first regaining her balance and strengthening her muscles. Each exercise was being doubled and tripled at her request, and she just kept going. Even if it hurt, even if it brought forth tears, she wouldn't stop! It looked like one of those scenes from a Rocky movie, except that this was real life.

Her tears were tears of strength, and her pain was a sign of healing. To watch her go, and to be the one she would lean on to assist her through this painful battle and one of the most trying times of her life, was truly a blessing. A miracle was taking place! We worked as a team, hand in hand, knowing that two were better than one.

One morning, I woke up to the smell of breakfast and hurried to the dining room. I couldn't believe what I was seeing!

There sat a plate of sausage, eggs, home fries, and toast! There was a napkin, silverware, and an empty cup for coffee.

I looked over at my wife who was sitting in her wheelchair, feeling shocked and puzzled because our kitchen was not wheelchair accessible.

She said, "Good morning! Sit down and eat before it gets cold."

I asked her, "How did you do this?" I began to reach for my coffee mug.

She said, "You sit down, and let me get that for you."

Still puzzled, I sat down and, as I did, my wife stood up out of her wheelchair, walked towards me, grabbed the coffee pot, and filled my mug. She could now walk on her own again, making a full recovery!

The look on our baby girl's face, as she awoke to see her mother standing at her crib to pick her up for the first time in months, was a look that would be forever etched into my heart. We hugged and kissed, we cried, and we praised the Lord!

The doctors were astonished and left scratching their heads, but to us, the answer to her recovery was simple. Love knows no bounds and will stop at nothing to be made whole again! It truly was miraculous!

As we began to take back our life, I had yet another vision. In my vision, I saw a beautiful land filled with rolling hills and lush green grass with cows grazing in the sun. Further off in the distance, there was a view of mountain peaks cascading together.

I turned around to see what was behind me, and there sat a house, but I couldn't make out what it actually looked like except that I could see the windows.

As I walked towards it, I remembered looking behind the house. The grass was bright green, and there were beautiful, mature trees. I saw birds of every color chirping as if they were singing. It felt like paradise to me!

I snapped out of it as my wife nudged me, asking, "What just happened to you? I asked you a question and you didn't respond. Are you okay?"

I told her what I had just seen, describing it to her in great detail.

She said, "That sounds amazing! What do you think it means?"

At that point, I honestly had no clue, and neither did she.

The funny thing was, we already had plans to move out of town. While we had no idea where the journey would take us in the days to come, we were excited about the future and looking forward to getting a fresh new start while leaving the past behind us.

We were stronger than ever, having gone through these things together as our daughter and I became Mommy's number one fan. We learned a lot about what it takes to truly overcome an extremely tragic situation as a family. We began to count our many blessings, knowing that our lives had been spared for a purpose even greater than we both imagined.

Chapter 10

Opposite Directions

Moving day had come. We found a brick ranch-style home in a small town in Indiana. My wife loved it and had to have it. It was dated on the inside, but the structure was sound. She had a vision for the home and knew that all it needed was a little tender loving care. Lipstick and rouge was what we called it.

We applied fresh paint, laid new flooring, and updated the kitchen and bathrooms. We did the work ourselves, turning that home into a mini palace. It was beautiful, becoming everything that she had envisioned it would be!

As we settled into our new life, our daughter was growing up. She was so full of joy and laughter, and she loved to sing. She'd sing all throughout the day while she played or when she was skipping through the house. You could even hear her rehearsing in her room at times, as she planned to give us her own little debut. She had quite the voice!

Life was now quiet and peaceful. My other two children, then in their teens, would come over every other weekend for visits. My son was a football player, and my daughter was a cheerleader with a love for gymnastics. They had a lot of friends, some of whom would even come with them on their weekends with Dad. They had made quite the names for themselves as they represented their small hometown with style and grace. I have always been proud of their many achievements.

My wife and I made a lot of friends in the community, as I took a job for a well-known door company, and she started working as a sandwich artist. We became very active in the neighborhood—helping others, reaching lives, and filling any needs that we heard about.

We even took a trip to Alaska during this time, which was amazing. It was a state that my mother had always dreamed about visiting since it was on her bucket list of places to go. During our trip, we found out why. It truly is God's country! Alaska is extremely breathtaking, and I would highly recommend it as a state to visit.

Our lives were going great, and we were happy, but we started to feel like we were being called to move somewhere else. One reason was that we knew we would meet many others with whom we could share our story. So, we prayed on it, asking the Lord to lead us.

Although my wife loved our house, she felt strongly that we were to move, and that we were specifically being called to somewhere in the mountains. I felt the same way, so we put our house on the market just to see if it would sell. We were testing the waters, so to speak. As we did, our home sold—and fast.

We called the moving company to come pack our belongings and move everything to a storage unit in Hayesville, NC. We hadn't found another home yet, but our plan was to head to North Carolina to begin our search.

Once we arrived in the state, we looked everywhere for a new home—from the foothills to the high peaks. Nothing seemed to stand out to us, and we were getting discouraged. We began to think that we may have made a mistake by selling our home back in Indiana, but it was too late to think like that. We had to press on!

Weeks went by, and we still hadn't found anything. In a last-ditch effort, we found a new realtor who offered to show us a couple of properties within the tri-state area. We were looking deep within the Smoky Mountains, and the area was beautiful. We absolutely loved it!

We had already seen two properties and had one more left to see. At the first two houses, we knew right off the bat that they weren't for us. So, when we arrived at the last property, knowing that this could possibly be the end of our search in North Carolina, we felt a little reluctant while still remaining hopeful.

The listing showed that this last house had three bedrooms and two bathrooms and sat on a three-acre parcel. Its asking price was $79,900, which was well within our budget. We knew that the property hadn't had any interested buyers for quite some time.

As we pulled up to the property, my wife stepped out of the car, looked around, and immediately said to me, "This place is from the vision you had!"

Mind you, we hadn't spoken of that vision in four years. It was exactly what I had seen. I could now see the house, as it was no longer a blur and sitting right in front of me!

The backyard had lush green grass, beautiful mature trees, and different colored birds flying around and chirping. In the front, there sat a million-dollar view, rolling hills with cows grazing on them, and the high peaks of the mountains cascading together in the distance.

I couldn't believe what I was seeing, and neither could my wife! All I knew was that I had to talk to the Lord. As my wife and daughter went inside the house with the realtor, I took a walk around the property and began to talk to Him.

I said, "Lord, this is unbelievable, but here I stand. You led us here, and we have arrived. What will You have me do? How much should our offer be? How shall I structure this deal?"

He spoke and said, "Place your offer at $47,900. Put $15,000 down upon approval, and close in seven days."

As soon as I heard that, my wife came out of the house and told me, "We are going to make an offer! We are going to own this property!"

I asked her what she thought of the home, and she replied that she thought it was nice and would complement all our needs. Most of all, she was fascinated by the view, especially as she recalled the vision. It was stunning!

I told her that I was just talking to the Lord and explained to her what He instructed me to do.

She replied, "Donnie, what if we lose the opportunity to buy this place? That's well below the asking price!"

I told her, "Since God has brought us this far, we have nothing to worry about! After all, He already showed me this place in the vision."

My wife agreed, though with hesitation.

As I walked into the house to check it out, our realtor asked us what we thought of the place.

I told him that my wife and I loved it and wanted to make an offer. Of course, our daughter loved it, too.

He replied, "Great! What's your offer?"

I told him that it was going to be a cash deal with no banks, as I always knew cash was king. Then I looked at him with a straight face and told him, "Our offer is $47,900. We'll put $15,000 down upon approval, and the balance will be paid at the time of closing—in seven days."

He looked at me steadily and replied in an optimistic tone, "Well, that's an offer. I'll draw up the paperwork and contact the owner."

That night, my wife had a lot to say as she was still concerned about the offer we had just made. She asked me why I didn't just offer what the seller was asking. She was scared that the owner would be offended by the offer and call the deal in progress off without a counter.

I looked at my wife and said, "Trust in the Lord! Everything is going to work out exactly how He has planned it."

The next morning, our phone rang. It was our realtor.

He said, "Good morning, Donnie! I've got great news for you and your family—your offer has been accepted, providing you cover all closing costs."

It was settled! We wrote the check for the down payment and closed in seven days.

That was it! We now had the deed and the keys to our new home. So, we called the moving company to bring our belongings to us. We couldn't believe that our storage facility was only fifteen minutes away! Even our belongings had made it within close proximity to where our future house would be. The Lord truly had His hand on this and led us every step of the way.

As we settled in, I got a job as a CNC machinist, my wife began working as a cake decorator, and our daughter would soon be starting kindergarten. We met new people and made new friends. We became highly active in the community just like we did in Indiana. We continued to tell our story, sharing all we could with those we met, while once again filling the needs of others with our message of hope.

Our story had grown and was not just about me, my journey, and how we first met. It now included the story of our tragic accident and the miracles surrounding it.

We also got involved with several different local ministries—men's, women's, plus various shelters. Between family time and our jobs, our days were long—early to rise and late to bed. We didn't mind; in fact, we actually enjoyed life and loved to be a blessing to others.

However, things in our marriage were beginning to change. We started to grow apart. We both felt it and talked about it, agreeing to do our best to try and work things out, not only for our sake but also for that of our daughter.

After all, we loved each other, and we had been through so much together! Unfortunately, it seemed like the harder we tried, the worse it got. We thought a time of separation would help, so I moved out. My wife eventually did, too, moving closer to town. Meanwhile, our house was left with just our furniture inside, no longer feeling like a home.

Even this time of separation didn't help, and my wife began to miss her family back home. Around this time, she received a call that her grandmother had passed away. She and our daughter flew back home for the funeral. I offered to go with them to support her, but she insisted on going alone.

While she was there, she called me, talking about how sad it made her feel to now see her grandfather being all alone. She thought of me and what was happening in our marriage, wanting to make amends.

Our hearts were both into it, and we truly tried to reconcile. We worked hard at it, but we were still living apart since she wasn't ready to live as a family again. Meanwhile, our house still sat fully furnished without a family.

One day, I got a call from my wife since she wanted to see me and had something she wanted to tell me. She told me that she had been thinking and came to her final conclusion regarding the days ahead.

In short, she told me that it wasn't fair for us to keep trying to hang on. We had to let go of each other and trust God for the outcome. With tears streaming down her face, she then told me that she wasn't called to marry a pastor.

I was confused by this since I wasn't a pastor yet, and that would only prove to come true much later down the road. Regardless, without a funny movie quote or even a punchline, her decision was final.

It felt like a door had been slammed shut with her on one side and me on the other. Our paths now took us in two opposite directions.

After that, she divorced me and moved back home. It crushed me, and it crushed her as well.

I kept asking myself, "Where did we go wrong? How could this happen, and why?"

I missed her and my daughter. They were now almost nine hours away. I shed a lot of tears during this time and felt my heart aching continually. I was in anguish and deep sorrow.

So, I did the only thing I knew to do. I called upon the Lord, falling upon my knees as tears fell from my face.

I told the Lord that I didn't understand why any of this was happening. I told Him that we had tried, but that it just wasn't good enough. I told Him how much I loved her and how much I loved my daughter. I told Him how much I missed them.

I shared my hurt and my pain with the Lord, and I told Him how much I loved Him. I told Him that even though I didn't understand why all of this was happening, no matter what I was going through, I was still going to serve Him. I told Him that I trusted

Him and that I was going to praise Him in the midst of the storm, even in the midst of my anguish.

I also told Him how I felt lonely, and I asked Him where His church was, as it seemed that people just couldn't be bothered. I told Him how people going through real-life problems needed a place to go—a place where they could reach out to others in times of crisis, a place to find encouragement, and most importantly, a place where they could pray one for another.

I told the Lord that my heart was once again broken and cried out to Him, "Fix it, Jesus!"

He replied, "My son, your heart is not broken, only wounded, for no man can undo what I have already done. We will get through this together, for I have never left you nor have I forsaken you. I love you!"

As I fell asleep, I had a dream where I was talking to the Lord. I had great concern for others who were in my kind of situation and for others who were in crisis. I had a deep desire to reach the needs of others, but I didn't know how other than to continue what I was already doing in the community.

The Lord spoke to me and said, "Out of great anguish and deep sorrow, true passion is born."

In the days ahead, the Lord would make my prayer for the people possible, I had no idea how it would work, but He showed me every step of the way.

We were now living in the days of the internet. Facebook and Twitter, now known as X, were right at my very fingertips. So, I started researching the possibilities of starting a website or a group page. I finally decided to start a Facebook group.

The name of it was going to be "Taking it to the Throne," which came from my having had that vision of His Throne Room years before. I knew the power it would have on those who sought prayer and brought requests to the only One who could answer them.

My mission was now inclined toward prayer and my statement of purpose was to gather prayer warriors who battle on their knees, praying without ceasing. The vision was simple—to connect lives, one soul at a time, one prayer at a time.

God made the impossible possible by connecting lives from all over the world! In fact, 1.6 million people joined the group from around the globe—

different nations and different tribes of every tongue were now connected, sharing their stories as they prayed one for another!

Through this group, the Lord answered my prayer, as it was a constant reminder and a double portion of the vision that He had given me years back when He told me that He had seen me many times. It was truly a blessing to my heart and soul.

I loved connecting with others, posting daily encouragement, sharing my story, and hearing the stories of so many others. I even started a 1-800 prayer line with other prayer warriors who remained on standby, willing to pray for the needs of others.

The best part of all was that Heaven was open for business twenty-four hours a day, seven days a week! As the sun would fall on this side of the world, it was already coming up on the other side of the world. The Lord was truly at work in the hearts of His people.

This wasn't about money, a job, or even fame, for that matter. In fact, I had a strict No Solicitation policy set in place on my group page. Anyone caught soliciting for any reason whatsoever was first given a warning. If it happened again, they were removed from the group.

My reason for that was simple, as it is written, "Freely we have received, and freely we shall give." There was no other reason besides that! After all, it doesn't cost anything to show kindness, it doesn't cost anything to show compassion, it doesn't cost anything to show mercy and grace, and it certainly doesn't cost anything to pray!

As word about the group continued to spread, I was called to be a guest speaker all across America. I often traveled to various speaking arrangements, meeting a lot of people on my journeys. Some were traveling like me, others were homeless, and still others were lonely and needed someone to talk to or just to lend them a listening ear.

I met people who wanted prayer and those who were dealing with addiction. Everyone had a need, whether or not they were willing to admit it. I discovered that what held a person back from asking for prayer was the level of comfort they felt about asking.

My passion for others was now a burning desire, and I felt that I just couldn't reach enough people! I constantly thought about those I met in person and the effect it had on me, and on them.

I thought to myself, "There has to be more!"

At that moment, I realized my calling. I had already spoken it. My passion was for the people. I wanted to meet so many more, I wanted to pray with them, I wanted to feed them, and I wanted to hug them and show them compassion. I had a burning desire to be the hands and feet of Jesus!

I looked up and said, "Here I am, Lord, send me!"

I had a genuine desire to reach the hearts of men, women, and children from all across the world. The best part about that was that it didn't come with a cost. It was a gift of God to His people!

As I've always said, "One act of kindness, one act of compassion, one handshake, one smile, one 'Hey, how ya doing?' can change a person's life!"

We never know what others are dealing with in their day to day. Just look at what I had been dealing with in my past, and nobody really knew how deep that pain was. I knew firsthand what a simple act of generosity did for me in my time of need, and I had the desire to be just like that person who once showed kindness to me!

Chapter 11

The Two Paths

My passion for the people continued to grow stronger, and my group page was also growing quickly. I met people from all over the world—places from Cape Town, South Africa, to Burroughs, Antarctica, and everywhere in between. I didn't even know that some of these places even existed!

People were messaging me left and right— twenty-four hours a day, seven days a week—just to talk, to share their stories, and to hear mine. Every story held its own significance in the journey that we each were walking. Every conversation was filled with love, hope, encouragement, and prayer.

I even heard testimony after testimony of prayers being answered—those who had been sick were now healed, those who once had addictions were now free, the families that had once been broken were now being reconciled, and those who had been lost were now found. Forgotten faith was now being remembered, and destroyed hope was finally being restored. Relationships were being built, one prayer at a time, and God was being glorified!

In my free time, I loved to go for hikes, just taking time for myself to ponder life and to pray. I love the outdoors, the scenic views, the smell of fresh pine trees, and, of course, nature itself.

I hiked many sections of the Appalachian Trail and met many through-hikers who also shared their stories and reasons about why they first chose to hike the 2,190+ mile trail. Every encounter started with a smile and ended with a hug or a handshake and a blessing for a safe and fruitful journey, and never ended without a prayer.

There was one place in particular that I absolutely loved to hike called Fires Creek. The trailhead started at the base of a beautiful waterfall, and its path wound alongside the falls. After hiking to the summit, which took roughly about forty-five minutes, one would hear the sound of water rushing down along the mountainside and could view the falls at various heights. Upon reaching the summit, there was a beautiful, almost calm, pool of water that collected from the streams that flowed into it and spilled over the cliffs to create the falls.

I would go there every day, just to talk to the Lord. It was my place of peace and solitude. As I would hike it, I would reminisce about the times my daughter and I would visit the recreational area.

She loved hiking and had a very adventurous spirit. She'd run ahead of me to smell the flowers, even picking some for me at times. She'd sing songs, and she'd talk about nature and her friends at school.

Every now and then, she'd stop to say, "Daddy, it sure is beautiful out here."

Once we reached the top of the summit, she couldn't wait to go back down. It was hot, humid, and muggy.

She'd say, "Boy, I sure am hot and sticky! Daddy, I feel icky!"

The closer we got to the bottom, she'd take off, skipping to the water's edge and dipping her toes into the basin of the falls. It's a well-known swimming hole.

She'd look at me as her foot now dangled in the water and say, "Daddy, please, can we?"

In response, I'd look down at her with a smile and say, "Well, whatcha waiting for?"

She'd scream, "Yippee!!" as she tore off her shirt, already having her bathing suit on underneath her clothes. Then I'd jump in—clothes, shoes, and all—just to seize the moment.

She'd laugh and say, "Daddy, you're all wet now!"

We would have a blast—splashing around, laughing, and enjoying the time we had together. After every hike, I always took her for ice cream before dropping her back off to her mom. My daughter was always a breath of fresh air as well as Daddy's Little Princess.

While hiking at Fires Creek, I prayed for my daughter and her mother. I prayed that the Lord would keep them safe and heal their hearts. I knew that our separation was tough on all of us. I prayed that somehow the Lord would always remind my daughter of how much I love her. She was only eight at the time of our split. I knew in my heart that He would, as He always had a way of reminding me just how much He loved me. After all, He's our Father, too!

One day, as I was hiking to the summit of the falls, I had been praying since I now felt a strong burden for those whom I hadn't yet met. After hearing the stories of those who joined "Taking it to the Throne" and talking to those whom I met in my travels, I began to think that personal encounters and experiences would serve a much greater purpose. It was much different than the virtual world that was already taking place in my life.

As I reached the summit, I sat down on a large rock facing the calm pool that rested at the mouth of the falls. I began to talk to the Lord, asking Him to explain to me why I was feeling the way I did about people I'd never met before.

At that moment the Lord appeared to me in another vision. We were standing side by side and He said to me, "I have set two paths before you. Choose which one you want to take."

As I began to look around, I saw both paths— one directly to my left and the other opposite it to my right. The one to my left had a narrow path that led to an old red church house—a very small building with a steeple on top in the same fashion as one of those one-room Southern-style chapels. Just off the sidewalk that went to the church house was a short path with lush green grass on both sides that led to a rampart overlooking the grandeur of the mountains. The sun was shining, and the skies were a majestic blue.

The path to the right looked dark and dangerous, yet mysterious and adventurous. The skies over this path looked gray and cloudy. I almost immediately knew what path I was going to choose.

I said to the Lord, "I'll take the path to my right," and I felt Him smile in response. This made me think that I made the right choice, although I somehow knew that whatever choice I made would be all right with Him.

He replied, "Know that I will be with you every step of the way."

As I started onto the path, it took an immediate dip and headed down a long, windy road. Then it got dark extremely fast. It rained and it stormed! Lightning was cracking and thunder was roaring!

I took cover underneath large plants with huge leaves. I even saw myself hanging off the edges of cliffs, climbing trees, and one-handedly holding onto branches of the trees I had climbed.

At times, it was downright scary! I'd call out to the Lord and say, "Are you there, Lord?"

He'd respond, "Fear not! For I am with you. Only be of good courage."

The path was extremely narrow, and the journey seemed to last forever. It felt like an obstacle course in the jungle. As I finally approached the end, I realized that I had returned to the exact place where I first started, now standing in front of the other path that had been to my left.

As the red church building with the steeple now stood before me, I decided to go over there and check it out. When I opened the door to the small chapel, I expected to see a few pews and an empty building, but that's not at all what I saw!

As I walked in, it was as if I had entered a football stadium or coliseum—there was a great multitude of people, and every single one of them had their eyes lifted to heaven and their hands in the air, praising and praying to the Lord! I even noticed the silhouette of a young woman holding a baby as she, too, was giving praise to the Lord.

The Lord then spoke to me and told me, "The people you see are all those that you have made an impact on, leading them closer to Me."

He also told me that my journey was now almost over as we walked back outside. The Lord motioned for me to take the short walk to stand upon the rampart.

As I did, I remember falling to my knees on top of the rampart with tears streaming down my face, thanking Him for what He had accomplished in my life and in the lives of so many others. I thanked Him for never leaving me or forsaking me. I thanked Him for the message He gave to me to pass on to others.

I was in shock yet blessed beyond measure. I now knew what God was able to do in one man's life who just dared to believe, a man who was willing to take a leap of faith, a man who would fear not and faint not.

As I stood up and turned around to look back at the two paths, I noticed the shadow of a cross illuminating the sky right before me. It was the biggest cross I had ever seen! The vision was now over.

At that moment, I realized that God was writing my greatest Love story, and not just mine but a story for all mankind, knowing that what He did for me, He desires to do for all of you.

I started to have dreams of traveling—being in different bus stations, train stations, airports, various trails, and sidewalks. My dreams were extremely vivid. I would see certain people within these places, and the details about their clothing, their faces, and where they were sitting or standing really stood out to me. I heard the buzzing of the chatter as people talked and the announcements of arrivals and departures coming from the loudspeakers. It was as if I was actually there.

When I woke up from these dreams, I knew that my prayers were being heard and answered. I knew that the Lord was going to send me into His great harvest! I was excited since it was what I was praying for, and it was the only thing that would fill the need of my great desire which had now become my passion.

I thought about the people on my Facebook group, as I knew I was being called to go into all the world. Since my time would now be limited compared to the time I had previously spent there, I prayed about it, and I prayed for all of them. Then I wrote a post, letting them know that the Lord was using me in other ways and that I would be busy in the days to come, but I promised to check in on them periodically.

That was it! It was settled—I packed a small backpack with two changes of clothes, some snacks, and my Bible. I didn't know where I would sleep, how I would get from place to place, or how I would even eat. I had quit my job, sold my belongings, and was now without transportation.

I figured that I'd let Jesus handle all of those details for me, knowing that the very hairs of my head were all numbered and that my life was of more value than the sparrows that Jesus took care of. I believed that I was in good hands and had nothing to worry about. It was my job to "Fear not" and "Be of good courage" to continue on the path He had already set before me.

Just like that, I headed out the door, excited about my journey ahead. My plan was simple—I planned to hit every major city and every small town in between.

It was just as the Lord said unto the servant, "Go out into the highways and hedges, and compel them to come in that My house may be filled."

As crazy as that sounded, I did exactly that. I was determined to meet everyone and anyone I could to share my story with, and nothing was going to stand in my way.

The story is about a man who, even as a young boy, endured some of life's hardest tragedies. Each trial and tribulation he went through brought forth its own disadvantages.

He was a man who became so broken to his very core that he felt suicide was his only option.

A man who had come to the end of his own rope and almost to the end of his very own life.

A man who had now been rescued, saved, and redeemed.

A man who was given a second chance at life, not only for himself but for the sake of so many others.

A man who was given the passion and courage to rescue others in their own time of crisis, stopping at nothing to succeed and allowing nothing to get in his way.

Chapter 12

Commissioned

As I began to travel, I thought about my circle of friends and the advice they gave me. Some clearly saw the hand of God on my life and sent me off with a blessing, "Go with God; our prayers are with you!" Others couldn't understand why I sold all of my things to help people I did not know. Then there were those who thought I had completely lost my mind.

To me, it didn't matter. I had already been exposed to the genuine Love of God, the Grace and Mercy of God, and the Great Compassion of God. I had a burning desire, a passion to reach the hearts of men.

I had a story to share, a message of love, hope, faith, and courage to give. I had already been sharing my story. I had already been reaching out to others by being highly active in the different communities I lived and traveled in. I saw firsthand the impact my story had on the hearts and lives of so many others.

Since I was all alone now, nothing was holding me to any one spot. I had become able to live as I prayed, filling my strong desire to be with the people. I had met others and heard of their heartache, their hurt, their pain, their loneliness, and their despair. I saw what was taking place in all the lives of those who were now calling upon me. I knew it all too well, as I too dealt with it in my life many times over.

I even saw corruption beginning to take over the church—the seeker-friendly messages that tickled the ears of the listeners, a watered-down gospel that was now preached, the prosperity message that taught "if you only sow a seed." I saw men standing in the pulpit who called themselves pastors and were not pastors at all, pickpocketing the saints of God in the name of Jesus. These were ungodly men turning the grace of our God into lasciviousness.

I saw how the church hurt people who were entrusting others with their spiritual growth and their very personal needs. I realized how it had even hurt me personally, thinking back to when my now ex-wife had sought counsel from the "church" she attended. Their council recommended a temporary time of separation, which eventually broke up our family and led us to divorce. What kind of "church" was that?

The "church" as we knew it was no longer teaching unity—it was now teaching a message of "every man for himself" just disguised by fancy words as it brought forth division and sowed discord amongst all of its followers. I couldn't believe it, and honestly, it broke my heart.

I could only imagine how Jesus felt! I knew that when He walked the face of this earth, He too saw the same thing. He even fashioned a whip and began to flip tables over that were filled with the goods being sold in His Father's house.

This was not at all His plan for the people He created and loved! I knew in my heart that what was taking place had nothing to do with Him or the gospel He preached. I had to warn others!

I didn't want people to be deceived and fall prey just like I had been. I had to contend for the Word of God. I had to tell them that the "church" had now become the mother of harlots and the abomination of the earth. I had to tell them what God was revealing to me. I had to tell them what God had done for me and is continuing to do for me, and what He was sharing with me—that He, too, wants and desires to do and to share with you, as "God is no respecter of persons, but in every nation, he that feareth Him and worketh righteousness is accepted with Him."

That was my message, and that's exactly what I delivered to the people as I began to set foot in many small towns and cities. While I traveled throughout the United States, it became very clear to me that the need for love, hope, and truth was infinite.

Many became hurt from their affiliations with the "church," while those who didn't associate with a "church" endured crisis just like everybody else. To me, it didn't matter whether they did or didn't have a measure of faith. We all are humans, we all have a heart, we all go through trials and tribulations, and we all have a desire to connect with others.

I began to notice that everyone I talked with was familiar with different parts of the Bible and that everyone heard about Jesus. Whether or not they believed in Him was left completely up to them. That's called free will, which I wasn't there to take away. Instead, I was there to meet each person in their time of need or moment of crisis. I was there to share my story while offering love, hope, and truth. I was there to give compassion through a display of genuine kindness, which manifested in many different ways.

As I made contact and had personal encounters with people, sharing my life experiences and hearing about theirs, I found that these people came from all different walks of life. Some were professionals in their fields, others were husbands and wives, many were homeless, others were widows, and some were orphans. It didn't matter to me who they were—if you had breath in your lungs and were still breathing, I was there to help you in any way that I could.

I met new people all the time as I walked into towns and cities, going through the parks or sitting on a bench to take a break and to just enjoy a beautiful day. I also met people in the bus stations, train stations, and even the airports, too.

As for the people who stood out to me from my dreams, yes, I met them too. Everyone I encountered just happened to be people you see every day—possibly your friends, possibly your neighbors, possibly your family, but even more so, possibly even you.

You see, the ones in need are people just like you and me. We all have a lot in common and more than one would think. It doesn't matter who you are or what you do for a living, we all have gone through trials. We've all gone through heartache and pain, just some of us more so than others. What makes us different is how we choose to handle the problems and situations that always seem to arise in our day-to-day.

Some choose to bottle it up.

Some choose to ignore it and pretend like it didn't happen.

Some choose to sweep it under a rug.

Some choose to shut down completely and close themselves off from their friends and family.

Some choose to self-destruct.

Still others choose to stand their ground and continue to battle whatever may come their way.

I, too, chose to react in many of these same ways.

We also find ourselves looking for answers to some of life's toughest crises. Whether or not we ask the questions aloud, the questions are still there, burdening our very souls. Yet, we've all been given a spirit to overcome and conquer. That's where the internal conflict we all deal with comes in. It's not an easy subject to talk about because it exposes our insecurities and weaknesses.

The problem arises when we begin to feel like nobody cares or that others are too busy with their own lives, and we don't want to become a burden or a bother to them. We begin to lose hope and, when all hope is lost, we find ourselves all alone, consumed in our own internal sea of despair. Our hearts become wounded, left without healing, which begins to manifest itself in very negative ways.

As I met many in my travels, there were a lot of things that no one could deny—there was power in prayer, healing found in companionship, joy that brought laughter, disgrace being exchanged for grace, and forgiveness being found in mercy. Also, not forgetting to mention, every conversation ended with a warm embrace in the form of a hug or a simple handshake and a million-dollar smile to enlighten their day. Each person was thankful that we had somehow crossed paths.

The mere fact that one person was willing to sit down to listen and talk with them made all the difference in the world. Knowing that someone whom they had never met before cared enough about them to be there for them in their time of need made an impact on their heart.

I truly resonated with the stories I heard. I was one of them, understanding the turmoil they were going through. At times, I just sat and listened to them, speaking not a word. I was no longer bringing the message but hearing a message. It touched my heart in very profound ways.

In my personal time, I always prayed for each and every person. I thought about them and their stories, hoping that no matter where they were in their lives they were okay. I knew that prayer had a way of making all things possible.

Love has many different languages and is shown in many different ways. Yet when it is truly felt, fervent Love casts away all fears, disperses all doubts, and covers a multitude of sin. Having the ability to display a passionate intensity of love, grace, and mercy for the sake and well-being of others goes beyond the human concept of any earthly love that we have ever known. It is a spiritual love that can only be described as divine.

This is the same love that kept Jesus on the cross until that final moment when He declared, "It is finished!"

This calling had now become my life, and it was such a blessing to me. I now had a need, and my need was to be with the people. It didn't matter if I was sleeping under bridges or under a box truck out in the middle of a field during a thunderstorm.

I had now given up my life for this very cause. Plus, I had the greatest Friend ever—One who stuck closer to me than a brother. I realized that the needs were greater than I had ever expected and bigger than anything I could have ever imagined.

Yet, there had always been a job posting for the calling that read, "The harvest truly is plenteous, but the laborers are few. Pray ye therefore the Lord of the harvest, that He will send forth laborers into His harvest!"

I'm sure that many have seen and read this notice, possibly not thinking much of it. To me, it was the greatest opportunity of a lifetime. Plus, the benefits were out of this world!

I personally never took note of this job posting myself, but it was exactly what I had been praying for. I now had a job for life, knowing that "No man, having put his hand to the plough and looking back, is fit for the kingdom of God." There was no turning back!

Meanwhile, I was continuing to get calls across the United States from people I had met on my Facebook group page, as they stayed up to date on what I was doing. They always filled me in on what was taking place in the group, mentioning that they noticed that the number of people who joined was falling fast ever since I was no longer able to spend as much time online. Honestly, I didn't know what to think about that, but I continued to pray for everyone there and only hoped that they were following the same great calling that was driving me.

When different people called me, they often asked me to come to their cities or towns to share my story with their neighborhood. Some offered to pay my travel expenses, others offered room and board. They knew I was a guy who would never accept a handout or be found holding up a sign on the streets. So, instead, they offered me work in my spare time and paid a fair wage.

I then used the money I made on travel expenses, meals, and coffee for those whom I met along the way. I bought supplies to build care packages, filled with a Bible, some snacks, gift cards to restaurants, socks, gloves, and scarfs. I passed these packages out as I traveled as a way to bless others, which often opened the door to conversation, which in turn always led to prayer.

As I visited many different areas, I continued to build relationships. People trusted me with their deep secrets, and they knew I wasn't going to go and tell others. As far as they were concerned, it was always between me, them, and the Lord.

Some people even wanted to get baptized but never felt right about being required to join a particular church before doing so. They were correct, so if they asked, I was willing and able to baptize them, as a body of water was never hard to find. It didn't matter if it was spring, summer, fall, or even winter. As long as the water hadn't frozen over and they didn't mind the cold water, neither did I.

There were times I even got arrested because I didn't know the various laws of each state. All of the charges were minor misdemeanors, but some were jailable offenses. I was usually out within twenty-four to thirty-six hours.

I knew that each arrest was merely Satan's attempt to stop me, to shut me up, and to discourage me, but that's not at all how it went down!

Maybe he didn't get the memo—I still had a voice, I still had a story to share, and I just landed in one of the most fertile spots to plant some seeds. After all, we are all men of the soil.

These men had already been thinking long and hard about their lives and their actions that landed them on the inside. They were dying for encouragement and longing to be heard.

Don't get me wrong—jail is no picnic. There are certainly those whose hearts have been hardened and definitely did not like to hear what I was preaching. Even the ones who acted tough and hard, however, I'd catch listening to what I was sharing with others.

Satan really messed up on that deal! Where else could one go here in America that would provide a roof over your head, a daily shower, three hots, and a cot—all while sharing the Love and Power of Jesus Christ?

As I shared my story, the men shared theirs. I even held daily Bible studies for whoever wanted to come. Most importantly, I had the opportunity to pray with these men. Some of the ones who initially came off as hardcore eventually showed up to ask for prayer. Even the guards asked me to pray for them, and when I stood before the judges, they apologized for my stay and always released me within an hour, saying, "God be with you."

You see, Satan couldn't stop me, and hell couldn't hold me! I was merely delayed in my travels while making the most out of my time by sharing with those who had been locked away from society itself.

It seemed as if the second I walked out those doors, I was immediately being swept off to my next destination. I felt like a stone being skipped across a glassy pond.

I began to realize that everything I had gone through in life was for a reason—it had a purpose and played a crucial role in my ability to entreat and speak with others. I could now speak to those who had addictions. I could now speak to those who had lost loved ones. I could now speak to those who felt alone and in despair. I could now speak to those who had been in jail. I could now speak on many different levels, having been there and done that myself.

I now had a much deeper personal understanding that came from experience and would continue to go with me wherever I went. Everyone I encountered could see it in me. When I spoke, I always spoke from my heart, and people respected that.

Growing up, I had always been taught to never judge a book by its cover—in other words, to never judge someone based on their past. It wasn't my job to do that since judgment was best left in the hands of God. Instead, it was my job to learn from it—both the good and the bad—and view it as a chance for growth while using what I learned as an opportunity to teach right and wrong.

I've always felt that just because some choose not to believe in Jesus, it doesn't give those who do believe in Him the right to turn their back on those who don't. After all, we've all been lost a time or two in our lives. We were all created in His image and His likeness. Those who chose not to believe in Him are the very people we need to show love to. Jesus truly died for us while we were still sinners.

The calls kept coming in from as far south as Texas and as far north as Maine—and everywhere in between. I seemed to be getting called back to New York State a lot. There was always a need everywhere I traveled, but for some reason, the city of Albany always weighed heavy on my heart.

Chapter 13

A Generation of Promise

My travels took me back and forth to Albany, NY, many times. In that time, my work on the streets, within the communities, and in the homes of many people was being noticed. I always offered to pass my phone number and email along to those who wanted to stay in contact. They often asked me if I had my own church, wanting to come and check it out for themselves.

I explained that the building wasn't the church, but that we the people are the church. My calling was to be with the people on the streets, within homes, and in communities. Some asked if I could refer them to a house of worship, somewhere they and their family could learn more about the Bible while connecting with others.

At the time, I didn't know of a place, as I was traveling far and wide. In addition, I was extremely cautious when sending others into the "church of today," which included myself. Instead, I told the people who asked that I would do my research and get back with them, as I knew that I would see them again.

As I gave the research my due diligence, I came across one place by the name of Reach Out Fellowship, run by Pastor Jerry Lynn. His mother had founded the church, being dedicated to reaching the lives of others. She also had a passion for missionary work. I knew in my heart that we shared the same passion.

Pastor Jerry was a teacher of the Word, taking it line by line. He, too, was dedicated and a man with a passion. He loves the Lord and His people.

Although I had neither met Pastor Jerry yet nor been to one of his services, I felt in my heart that his church was a place where I should send people if they asked. As I did, those people started attending his services.

The congregation there was small, so any new faces were definitely recognized and welcomed. Pastor Jerry stood at the door at the end of every service, shaking people's hands while thanking them for coming. For those who were new to Reach Out, he would ask if they enjoyed the service and then ask how they had heard about him, as he also broadcasted his teachings over the radio.

Well, the people I sent his way told him all about me. Of course, Pastor Jerry didn't know who I was, so he asked where I was and stated that he wanted to meet me.

At the time, I was off in another state, hard at work. I began receiving calls from those who now attended his church, inviting me to come and meet Pastor Jerry. They explained that he was not only curious but eager to finally meet me.

So, as soon as my work was finished in that location, I took the next train back to Albany to finally attend one of his services. The funny thing is, Pastor Jerry didn't know I was coming, and neither did anyone else. Although my train was delayed, it arrived in time for me to catch a bus and take the short walk to his service.

As I stepped into the building quietly, I realized that I was just a few minutes late. Pastor Jerry had already started the service. The people who knew me motioned for me to come and sit next to them. Of course, since it was a small congregation, everyone couldn't help but notice me, including Pastor Jerry.

He looked at me, gave me a smile, and said, "Welcome," before going on with his service. As I watched him teach, I knew that his curiosity about me was getting the best of him. Yet, since he was always at the door at the end of every service, he knew that he would have the opportunity to talk with me.

After the service ended, I finally had the chance to meet Pastor Jerry and introduce myself. He's a very sweet man with a very gentle spirit. Of course, he wanted me to hang out for a while and tell him all about myself. So, I did.

We talked for a good while, and he also invited me to attend his mid-week prayer meetings. If there was one thing I needed, it was prayer. Prayer had become a huge part of my life, not just for myself but for the many others I had been reaching out to. I figured, the more prayers going up, the more blessings coming down.

As I attended prayer meetings and more services, Pastor Jerry and I became good friends. He even had work for me to do around his house and at the church. He took me out for coffee, breakfast, and lunch, which gave us more time to get to know one another and hear all about what the Lord was doing—not only in Albany but everywhere I had been as well.

One day, Jerry asked me to make time in my schedule to meet him and his wife for dinner. He had something on his heart and wanted to talk with me about it.

So, I went to meet them at a Greek restaurant. I had never eaten Greek cuisine before but was very curious to try it out.

As we ate, Jerry explained to me that he had been praying for me. He felt the very important need to ordain me and even felt that God was calling him to do so.

In response, I explained to him that I didn't feel like I needed to be ordained by a man because it was God, and God alone, who called me, chose me, and ordained me for such a time as this.

I reminded Pastor Jerry of a Scripture in John 15:16 that read, "Ye have not chosen Me, but I have chosen you, and ordained you, that ye should go and bring forth fruit, and that your fruit should remain: that whatsoever ye shall ask of the Father in My Name, He may give it you."

Jerry completely agreed with me. If there was one thing we agreed on, it was the Word of God. Yet, he and his wife explained to me that, in this day and age, if I wanted to reach more people in New York State, being ordained with a pastor's license would only open more doors to reach others.

We continued to eat dinner and talk. By the way, the food was amazing. As I pondered on these things, I was also asking God if this was the direction that He was leading me in.

Jerry further explained his plans and suggested a date for my ordainment. Then the three of us held hands and prayed. At that point, I was now at peace with the idea and accepted his invitation. I was ordained on March 27, 2016. It was a beautiful ceremony.

A few weeks later, during one of Pastor Jerry's services, he opened up a time for anyone in the congregation to share a testimony or ask for prayer.

I had already built relationships with everyone who attended, and they always asked me questions about what it was like to do what I was doing. I was always happy to tell them, finding them excited to hear my news as they expressed that they wanted to be a part of the work in any way they could.

As I was sitting there, listening to others share their testimony and asking for prayer, I felt something come over me. I don't really know how to explain it other than to say that I felt lightheaded like I was in a fog.

The very moment the last person finished speaking, I stood up and gave an invitation. I welcomed anyone and everyone who was willing to join me to come out with me and take part in the work I was already doing. The need was there, the laborers were few, and the more people I could get involved the better.

Just like that, another prayer was answered. Fire First Ministry was born. The Lord had opened another door and this time we had laborers. Rain or shine, snow or ice, the work never stopped. We continued on, twenty-four hours a day, seven days a week.

It's important to note that Fire First Ministry was not associated with any one church or organization. We were merely a group of individuals from various communities who had a passion and desire to serve others. The work was completely self-funded, supported through the hearts of generosity and donations of everyone who took part.

Whether or not you belonged to a church didn't matter to us. If you were willing to help others, you were welcome to join us. We knew that everyone had a unique story of their own to share that would truly benefit the lives and hearts of others. Those who had a need for whatever reason no longer had to wait for help or wonder if a board would find their request deserving of assistance.

Let's face the facts—asking for help is never easy. I know firsthand what it feels like. You feel like you're being backed into a corner with only two options—the first is to run and get out of there fast, while the second is to be stuck sharing personal information that's near and dear to your heart with someone who truly doesn't care, knowing you are just another number within their many case files, just another unfortunate story seeking help. It's embarrassing, to say the least, and most people would rather not ask than suffer the humiliation.

With Fire First Ministry, there was no building to go to, no lines to stand in, no forms to fill out, and no phone calls to make. We weren't there to pry into anyone's business, and we weren't there to take away anyone's free will. If they chose to share their story with us or pray with us, that choice was completely left up to them.

No matter what, real needs were met on the spot. We called directly to Heaven for the Lord's assistance as He Himself heard the prayers of His people and poured out His blessings regardless of what time of day it was.

As I began to take teams out into the streets within the communities, the outpouring and desires of these volunteers began to grow. Those care packages I had previously built on my own were doubling and tripling, both in size and in volume. Many volunteers were helping me put them together, thinking about the lives that would be blessed as they worked alongside me.

When the teams saw the needs for themselves, they began to buy their own supplies—Bibles, blankets, food, socks, hats, gloves, toothbrushes, toothpaste, and whatever else they had seen a specific need for. They, too, had found a purpose for their own lives, and it even brought forth a form of healing as they truly learned what is meant by the verse, "It is better to give than to receive."

Obviously, at this point, the ministry was growing as word traveled all over Albany and throughout the greater Capital District. New people were signing up to volunteer, with some even coming from as far as New York City. It took a lot of hands to run a ministry of this size and the Lord had the right people in place.

One of those individuals was Sister Sadelle who originally was from Ireland. She was extremely passionate in prayer and had a desire to fill the needs of others. In turn, she introduced me to a friend of hers named Vida who also had a passion for people and loved being involved with various street ministries.

Vida was from Albany and had many different connections, so we teamed up and I asked her to become the co-founder of Fire First Ministry. She was excited and readily agreed. As we worked together, Vida asked me if I held proof of being ordained as a pastor, which I did. She explained that it would be an essential key to helping us access certain places where we could bless the people, reminding me how the Lord had been guiding and directing my every step for His specific purpose.

Before I knew it, we were holding monthly events in multiple locations throughout the Capital Region. At the senior citizens' homes, we spent time with seniors, talked with them, listened to them, prayed with them, served them drinks, and played games with them.

At the shelters for women and children, we set up several fun activities for the children while inviting the mothers to take part as well. We even dropped off donations of clothing, toys, and more while we were there.

In the summer, we held back-to-school drives, passing out backpacks that were filled with all of the supplies that a child would need for their first day of school.

I was also called to the hospital on several occasions. I prayed with and for those who were sick and dying, bringing peace and comfort to the patients and their families.

Fire First Ministry truly became essential to everyone involved. We received calls and thank you cards from individuals and families who had been blessed by the passion and generosity of the volunteers.

As co-founder, Vida demonstrated that she was not only great with people but also had a skill in filling administrative needs. Being a writer of sorts, she would help me send out monthly newsletters that came with pictures to keep the community updated on the work of the ministry.

We both believed that we were doing all things for the Lord, agreeing never to ask for money. After all, God was already supplying all of the needs according to His riches and glory, giving us the keys to the kingdom that unlocked doors which had not been opened to me before.

Various organizations and businesses heard about our efforts and began to give us many donations from socks and coats to food and bottled water, and everything in between. We now had volunteers at bus stations, train stations, city parks, and neighborhood centers loaded with all of the tools they needed to reach out to others.

All the while, I was down at the city mission several days a week. Something always needed to be done there, so it became a part of our event planning. I was regularly in touch with their volunteer coordinator since the mission needed to know how many volunteers were going to be showing up each day to lend a helping hand. If there were openings, Fire First was filling those slots.

Sometimes, we received so many donations that we planned events to pass them along. We held them in a parking lot directly across the street from the city mission. Once the word got out that we were on the streets and filling specific needs, it didn't take long at all for people to start showing up. Every person was greeted with a smile, a handshake or warm hug, and a prayer.

Meanwhile, across the street, I noticed that a food truck had pulled up. The owner came over to let us know that anyone who was hungry could stop by. He was making hamburgers and hotdogs, served with a bag of chips and a drink—all at no charge. All were welcomed as long as supplies lasted!

I even took teams into NYC to do exactly what we were already doing. As we walked throughout the city, we noticed that there were others who were doing the same thing. Each person had their own story that was filled with a message of love and hope.

Our message was well received everywhere, from the streets to homes, as we even knocked on people's doors to bless them. When someone answered our knock, they always enjoyed the conversation, the gift bag we passed along, and the prayers.

We weren't there to ask them to join a church or to become a part of a particular denomination. We were just there to let them know that somebody cared. We were willing to talk to them, lend a helping hand, and of course pray for them.

Back on the streets, we were ministering to and building relationships with certain people. I noticed that they were no longer asking for care packages, as they knew that blessing was coming. Instead, they were specifically asking for prayers, which were almost never for themselves. No, in fact, they were asking for prayers for their family members, their friends, and all others who were homeless and in need, just like them.

During this time, Sister Sadelle planned a trip back to Ireland to visit family and friends. She invited Vida and me to go along, as she intended to visit some churches while back home. While I already had my hands full with the work that stood before me, Vida jumped on the invitation and purchased her ticket to go.

While Vida and Sadelle were in Ireland, they began to tell others about Fire First and the work of the ministry. They shared with people what the Lord was doing back in America, which made many people excited. I started to get emails from pastors and others who had heard all about it. The emails expressed how the message of love and hope brought excitement to them, giving them a zealousness to keep on persevering with the work that they themselves had started. They also shared how they were sending prayers for the work of Fire First while in return asking that we pray for them as well, which we gladly did.

As the word spread, not only throughout parts of the northeast but even to Ireland, we all remained humble. It was never about fame, and it definitely was not about fortune. It was never about me or anyone else who was involved. The focus always remained on God and His unfailing Love for His people.

You see, what was actually taking place wasn't something you'd see on TV as you flipped through the channels, coming across a large auditorium filled with a multitude of people listening to one man grandstanding and talking about a God he did not know. Nor was it about the infomercials you'd see as ungodly men pedaled their books of prosperity with promises to get you rich or offered you a flask of miracle water to buy that would change your life.

Heck, if you really wanted miracle water, all you had to do was walk to your kitchen sink and pour yourself a glass from the faucet. After all, we all need water to live, and life itself is the greatest miracle of all.

I knew what the Word of God said about false teachers and false prophets and how "the time has come that judgment must begin at the house of God," and "if it first begin with us, what shall the end be of them that obey not the gospel of God?"

You see, the church had gone astray and many had no idea what the actual church of Jesus Christ was intended to look like. Even now, many have no clue. Biblically, the church is not a building made by man's hands.

Instead, it's a people who have a strong desire to BE THE CHURCH—a people who desire to live in unity with one hand helping the other as all needs are being met, a people with genuine concern for God and country, a people who aren't afraid to step outside the confines of their homes to entreat and serve others. That's what the true church of Jesus Christ is all about!

One certainly does not have to get all gussied up on a Sunday and drive to a building to listen to a meeting that will only cost money and time. Neither is it about listening to a man who has made up his own doctrine in an effort to fill his own pockets, completely disregarding the needs of so many others.

As a matter of fact, the church of the New Testament—a people—met in various homes to pray, share Scripture with one another, and eat a meal together. And that was what actually was taking place back home and on the streets.

The example that we set forth was a picture of what Jesus's true church was intended to look like, knowing that the Kingdom of God had truly come unto us. We were a collective group of people who sought to fulfill the Will of the Father. We were a people with a desire to reach the hearts of one another—one blessing at a time, one prayer at a time, and by any means necessary. As it is written, "A chosen generation, a royal priesthood, an holy nation, a peculiar people, that we should shew forth the praises of Him who hath called you out of darkness into His marvelous light."

Our passion was to watch people begin to serve one another and to entreat others they did not know with love, compassion, grace, and mercy. It was truly a sight to behold. Not only was it a blessing to take part in for everyone from all different walks in life but it was also another free Gift of God.

Can you imagine what the world would look like if others would only do the same? The world would truly become a better place as we lived according to how God intended us to live, now on earth as it is in heaven. Life would truly be about showing love and compassion to others, not just to our family and friends but to so many others whom we do not know.

Jesus Himself explained it to us all in such simple words that even a young child could understand it.

"For I was an hungered, and you gave Me meat; I was thirsty, and you gave Me drink; I was a stranger, and you took Me in; Naked, and you clothed Me; I was sick, and you visited Me; I was in prison, and you came unto Me."

Then shall the righteous answer Him, saying, "Lord, when saw we Thee an hungered, and fed Thee? Or thirsty, and gave Thee drink? When saw we Thee a stranger, and took Thee in? Or naked, and clothed Thee? Or when saw we Thee sick, or in prison, and came unto Thee?"

And the King shall answer and say unto them, "Verily I say unto you, inasmuch as ye have done it unto one of the least of these My brethren, you have done it unto Me."

The Lord also left us with instructions on how He would fulfill His promise to mankind with our help, saying,

"Bring ye all the tithes into the storehouse, that there may be meat in Mine house, and prove Me now herewith," saith the LORD of hosts, "if I will not open you the windows of heaven, and pour you out a blessing, that there shall not be room enough to receive it!"

As we worked the streets of Albany, everyone's prayers were answered, and none went without. There was no need too great or so little that Jesus could not fill it. He truly is the God of more than enough! Hope was being restored into each and every heart of those we encountered.

Chapter 14

Mr. Ellis

A s one can imagine, I had very little time for a personal life at that time. The long days turned into weeks, months, and years. It started to take its toll on me, but I always remained positive, peaceful, and pleasant. Others would often ask about me, as they, too, saw my fatigue.

I would always say, "Thank you for asking, but there's no need to worry about me. If there's one thing I know, it's that I'm gonna be all right."

Yet, deep down inside, I felt that if I needed and wanted anything, it would be a friend—someone whom I could talk to and hang out with outside of the circle that encompassed my life.

So, I prayed about it. I figured it couldn't hurt to ask, and in the worst-case scenario, I'd just keep on keeping on. After all, I was happy, loving life, and taking care of the needs of others.

One day, I was over at a neighbor's place. His name was Mr. Charles. He was a jolly old chap who always had something that needed fixing, and I always did what I could to help him out.

This time, he wanted a ceiling fan installed in his kitchen. I knew how to do it, and I was glad to do it for him. As I was installing the fan, a man came walking through the front door, just a-cussing like a sailor. I kept quiet and continued my work.

Mr. Charles looked at his friend and said, "Have ya met Pastor Donnie?"

At that point, the man looked shocked, dropped his head in shame, and walked back outside to grab some things from his car. That man was none other than Mr. Ellis.

You see, he and Mr. Charles work at the same company in Albany, delivering asphalt and various other products all over the northeast. As I later found out, Mr. Ellis lives in the Champlain Valley and would stay with Mr. Charles during his work week to cut down on his travel time to and from work.

As Mr. Ellis came back inside, he had his own job to take care of—repairing Mr. Charles's kitchen faucet. He walked into the kitchen and looked up at me as I stood on the stepladder installing the new ceiling fan.

He said to me, "Do ya mind if I step around you?"

I didn't mind, stepping down to shake his hand and properly introduce myself. "I'm Donnie. It's nice to meet you."

I could tell he was a little embarrassed since he has the utmost respect for clergymen.

He looked at me and asked, "Are you really a pastor?"

I looked back at him and replied, "Well, that's the rumor."

We got a good chuckle out of that one, and he emphatically apologized for his language. I told him it was no big deal and not to worry about it, as I understood.

"Some days are better than others," I told him.

Mr. Ellis smiled as he got to work on the faucet.

We seemed to hit it off right off the bat, as he took note that I, too, was just an average, ordinary guy like everyone else. He and I would become very close friends.

Mr. Ellis and I would talk just about everything under the sun. He was very interested in the work I was doing in the greater Capital District and wanted to know more about both it and me. Likewise, I was curious to know more about him. He just had a way about him, being the kind of guy you looked at and could just tell that he'd been through some stuff, the kind of guy with a lifetime of experience just waiting to be told.

Believe it or not, despite our first encounter, Mr. Ellis has a very gentle and caring spirit. He puts the needs of others before his needs. He's got jokes and loves to laugh. He's hard-working—and when I say hardworking, I'm not putting that lightly. He's old-school and takes pride in everything he does. He's the kind of guy you look up to and one who can teach you a thing or two about life.

I was excited to get to know him. Whenever I had the free time, I'd stop by Mr. Charles's just to hang out with both of them. They enjoyed sitting outside on the front porch, talking shop after a long day at work. I always enjoyed listening to their conversations, always having something to add to it.

Another thing about Mr. Ellis is that he's a man of many hats. There's nothing that man can't do. He's always wrenching on something, and I enjoyed doing the same, too, so I was always glad to lend him a helping hand.

Mr. Ellis came to understand my work within the community, and I knew that he was always looking to help others out as well. Come to find out, he and his wife were doing some spring cleaning back home. Instead of throwing everything away, he brought me an entire truckload of supplies from around his house that he knew would help others out. Also, whenever he had time, he'd always come find me and give me a helping hand when I was working in the neighborhood.

The work we did for the neighbors wasn't easy. We mowed lawns, cleaned swimming pools and gutters, and even cut down trees—and lots of them. There was no job too big or too small that Mr. Ellis and I couldn't handle.

We often looked at each other with big grins on our faces after being asked if we could do certain things. You see, the neighbors often thought they'd have to pay big money for what they wanted to have done, and they had no idea what the two of us were really capable of.

"Child's play," we'd chuckle with a knowing wink at each other. Then we'd tell the neighbors that it wouldn't be a problem to complete their job, normally having it done within a day or two. When we finished, we never charged them a dime. We were just glad to be of service to them.

It seemed like the better we got to know each other, the more we were a lot alike and yet still different in our own special ways. Mr. Ellis is twenty years older than me, and there was nothing that stood in his way when it came to helping others out. He was exactly what I had been praying for—and so much more.

One day, we were talking, and I asked him about what his life was like back home. Come to find out, he had a farm with horses, chickens, cows, and a German shepherd. Mr. Ellis even made his own hay. He had all of his own farm equipment and a collection of antique tractors that he actually used quite often. Each tractor had its own special purpose in maintaining the farm.

Mr. Ellis also explained that there was always something to do at home, but he just never had the time to get it all done.

I said to him, "Well, Mr. E., if you would ever like a helping hand, I'd be glad to help you."

Not long after that, Mr. E. hatched a plan to take me back home with him over a three-day holiday weekend. He had a roof to replace over his carport and three large fields that needed haying. I was excited and glad to oblige.

Well, the day came to take the trip up to his house—a two-and-a-half-hour journey into the high peaks of the Adirondacks. We had been hanging out the night before, after a long week of work for both of us but had a plan to leave bright and early the next morning.

I, unfortunately, overslept and woke up in a panic. I looked across the street to see if he was still around, but his car was gone. I started to feel extremely bad and thought to myself that I would take a bus or train up to where he lived.

I grabbed my phone to call and apologize, thinking I had let him down, as well as to let Mr. E. know my plan to head up there on my own.

Mr. E. answered with, "Well, good morning, Mr. Donnie." He explained how he had tried to call, text, knock at my door, and even wait around until he could no longer wait anymore, thinking I may have changed my mind. So, he had already headed home but was only an hour away.

He could sense in my voice how bad I felt, so he turned his car around to come and pick me back up. He arrived, and then we were right back on the road.

During the trip, I kept apologizing for oversleeping, but Mr. E. understood and was just happy that everything was working out. After all, we had fields to hay and a roof to replace!

Once we arrived, I had the honor of meeting his wife, Mrs. Tina. She, by the way, had no idea that Mr. Ellis was bringing anyone home with him, and especially not a pastor.

She said to me, "You must have made quite the impression on Ellis—he never brings people back to his house. And he certainly doesn't wait around for people!"

She had already heard about me from Mr. Ellis while they spoke on the phone throughout the week. She was happy to hear that he had made a new friend, but she just hadn't expected to meet me any time soon—if ever.

After our formal introduction, Mr. E. and I headed out to his barn to start working on one of his tractors that needed a driveshaft replaced before we hit the fields in the morning.

That night, Mrs. Tina made a fine homemade meal—chicken dumplings, mashed potatoes, and a strawberry cake for dessert, which is Mr. E's favorite. Little did he know, it would soon become my favorite as well.

The food was so good that I had five plates before dessert. I had never eaten that much before, and Mr. Ellis knew it!

He just looked at Mrs. Tina and said, "I have never seen him eat this much before, but it sure does my heart good to see him enjoy it."

Mrs. Tina replied, saying, "Well, don't be shy! There's plenty more—and save room for dessert."

Honestly, I couldn't eat anymore. I was stuffed! But that strawberry cake sitting right in front of me would've been a shame to let go to waste. Besides, I had been brought up to eat everything that was put before me. Boy, I sure am glad that I tried it. Best strawberry cake ever!

The entire weekend went extremely well. We managed to get all three fields of hay cut, bailed, and put away. We even had time to replace the roof on the carport.

Mrs. Tina sure was glad that I came to lend a helping hand after all. She had now seen for herself what Mr. E. saw in me. She even welcomed me back, giving me an open invitation to come anytime I wanted.

"Ellis always has something to do around here, and he really enjoys your company," she was saying to us before we headed back down to Albany.

Truth be told, Mr. E. was always a breath of fresh air, and I always loved hanging out with him. He taught me a lot and has quite the story himself. Turns out, his wife, Mrs. Tina, is actually quite charming in her own special way, too.

As time went on, I made several trips up to Mr. E.'s house to help him with all the projects he wanted to get done. Although the project list often seemed endless and like it would take a lifetime to conquer, we always knocked the big jobs out first.

I eventually got to meet Mr. E's entire family. They're amazing people, each one different and special in their own unique way. In fact, Mr. E. and

Mrs. Tina always had family and friends coming and going, stopping by on their daily travels just to say hi, grab a cold drink or coffee, and eat a snack. I also met their many grandchildren who Mrs. Tina loves and adores.

As I somehow became a part of their wonderful family, I always knew that it was a place that I would always consider home and a gift that I would always cherish. In many ways, it reminded me of my parents' house when I was growing up with the people we had coming and going all the time. In the same way, no matter what Mr. E and Mrs. Tina had going on, they always laid out the red carpet for me when I went to see them.

On one of my many trips up north, I decided that I would tackle one of the biggest projects still on his to-do list—converting one of his buildings into a functional two-bay garage with plenty of open working space.

At first, the old garage was filled with everything imaginable—an old tractor, all the tractor equipment one could ever need, and a hodgepodge of random farm supplies. It also had a tool shop attached to it where Mr. E would keep all of his tools neatly and professionally organized. He had all the supplies to get the job done, from insulation to plywood. He just needed a helping hand.

As I was working on the reconstruction, I talked to one of Mr. E.'s close relatives, as she asked me what my plans were to do on the farm this time around.

I explained to her the plan to completely renovate the garage to make it the heart of the farm, which I was already in the process of doing.

She smiled, as it made her happy to hear about it, saying, "There's no one more deserving than Mr. Ellis!"

As you can see, I'm not the only one who thinks so highly of him!

Well, his two-car garage is now finished, complete with fresh paint, new shelving, a workbench, and an old wood stove he built many years ago to keep off the chill during the long, hard, cold winter months. Did I mention that Mr. E. is also an expert welder and tin-knocker?

As Mr. E. would say, it sure does my heart good to know that he now has a garage of his own to work in and tinker around in. He no longer has to repair farm equipment outside on the ground in the mud or in the snow and ice.

As a bonus, our conversations were always deep. Mr. E. and I talked about our lives and gave each other good, solid advice. I can tell him anything, as he isn't one to judge others, and he was able to do the same with me. I also enjoyed learning from Mr. E., finding him to be a jack of all trades, clever to say the least, and always having a few tricks up his sleeve.

Mr. Ellis is a pretty amazing guy and, if you were to ask my opinion about him, I'd say, "Everyone should have a Mr. Ellis in their life!"

Can you just imagine what I would have missed out on if I would have judged him the first day I met him? Just think about what I would have lost had I been one of those self-righteous, holier-than-thou people who think they're better than others

Just because I had a title in front of my name, it didn't mean that I was different than anyone else. Which, by the way, always felt weird to me when others would call me pastor. "Donnie" was just fine by me.

Mr. Ellis, however, seemed to find it funny when he introduced me to people who were caught up in the same situation that he had been in on the day we first met.

He would say, "Have you met my friend, Pastor Donnie?" And then he would get quite the chuckle out of the person's reaction.

I'm so glad that I've never been that kind of person. I would have totally missed out on having one of the greatest friends I have ever had the pleasure and honor of knowing, his family included. As far as Mrs. Tina goes, she never fails to tell Mr. E to ask me when I'm coming home. They're truly an amazing family!

It just reminds me of another well-learned lesson I first heard as a child—Never judge a book by its cover. One just never knows what story is being told or how the tale will unfold until you've read its many pages for yourself in its entirety. This was one story that I'm glad I didn't miss out on and was truly blessed to become a part of!

Chapter 15

Lake Waccamaw

I n the spring of 2020, an invisible and deadly virus called the coronavirus—otherwise known as COVID-19—was claiming the lives of thousands. It was taking place not just here in America but on every single continent all around the globe.

The whole world was now facing a silent killer. There was no cure and no vaccine to stop the rapid spread. Fear had now entered the hearts of many.

New laws were introduced to help curb the spread of covid. Face masks were now mandatory in every public place. A six-foot distance was required to separate one from another, and a shelter-in-place order was established. This meant that we were not allowed to leave our homes unless we needed groceries or prescriptions, or if we were helping someone who couldn't help themselves.

We were told how many people we could have in our home at one time—no more than ten. Any special events like weddings, funerals, holiday gatherings, and family get-togethers were no longer allowed. We were placed under a curfew. Anyone caught violating these laws was subject to stiff fines and even possible jail time.

As all of this was going on, Mr. Ellis and I talked and hung out every day during the work week when he was staying in Albany. We talked about what was going on back home in his neck of the woods, and I filled him in with what was taking place out on the streets.

Covid didn't stop me! There were still people who were homeless, people who had needs, and people who now wanted prayer more than ever.

Yet, things only seemed to get worse. Any future events that Fire First Ministry had scheduled for the senior citizens' retirement homes, women's and children's shelters, and hospitals were now canceled due to "public health and safety" reasons.

On the national front, U.S. Border Crossings were shut down, flights were canceled across the board, public worship services were no longer allowed, and schools and businesses alike were told to close their doors until further notice. Covid was considered to be a widespread pandemic all around the world.

One day, Mr. Ellis mentioned that it appeared to him that the doors in Albany were now closing to me. He knew that my Boss had other plans for me, which were much bigger than Albany itself.

I wasn't sure how Mr. E. knew all that, but it was true—I already had my bag packed and felt called to travel. Unlike 9/11, my feet were ready to hit the ground running. It was another answered prayer.

One of the last conversations we had while I was still in Albany was about his great concern for me. Mr. E. took note of how I spent my life taking care of so many people.

He asked me, "Who is there to take care of you?"

I responded, "Well, Mr. E., that's what the Lord is for. He's with me every day and always by my side. Plus, I now have you to talk to!"

He found my response to be kind, but it wasn't the answer he was looking for. He asked again, "Who's there to take care of you?"

I then told him that I understood what he was getting at and that while, in my heart, I wanted that special someone in my life, I just didn't think it would happen.

Think about it! With the lifestyle I was called to live—traveling all the time, never settling down, without a job working for the man that others found respective in today's society—the chance of me finding that special person was slim to none.

She would have to share my passion, and she would have to walk by faith and not by sight. She would have to endure scrutiny from family and friends. I didn't think such a woman existed. Even if she did, she'd have to be some kind of wonderful.

I explained to Mr. Ellis that I had prayed about it and left it up to the Lord. Whether the Lord decided to bring such a person into my life or not was completely up to Him. No matter what happened, I was going to continue my journey. I would simply remain alone if I had to. The lives of others have always been more important to me than my own life.

Mr. Ellis nodded and said, "Well, there's always hope, Mr. Donnie."

I couldn't agree more with him and was extremely touched by his concern for me.

A few days later, I left Albany and headed north to Portland, Maine. I began a new travel route that went through major cities and small towns all along the East Coast—from Portsmouth, New Hampshire, and Providence, Rhode Island, all the way to Charlotte, North Carolina, and even Montgomery, Alabama.

What I saw along the way as I arrived in each major city and small town was a picture that you'd see in some zombie apocalypse movie. America had become a ghost town!

The whole country was paralyzed by this virus. The streets were empty—no cars and no traffic—and businesses and churches were locked and chained. The only people who remained out and about were the homeless and less fortunate who had nowhere to go and were left to fend for themselves. All across the land, fear had taken over.

As I began to reach out to the people I saw within different camps along the way, I felt a sense of peace and calm without worry coming from those whom I met. Although we had no answer to what was really taking place, we knew Who did.

More than half of the people I met throughout the entire journey asked me to pray with them. The prayers they requested were not for themselves but for others—family members, friends, loved ones, people who were sick that they didn't know, and pretty much everyone around the world. Truth be told, we were even praying for you!

As we took each other's hands, they asked me to pray while they stood in agreement with me. Our prayers often went like this—

Dear Heavenly Father,

We come before Your Almighty Throne of grace and mercy. It is with a heavy heart that we come. Our prayers are not for ourselves but for those we love and for those we do not know—every man, every woman, and every child across the world.

Father, we know that Your Son, Jesus, was wounded for our transgressions, He was bruised for our iniquities, the chastisement of our peace was upon Him, and by His stripes we are healed.

Lord, this is our prayer for all Your people—restore our health, restore our hearts and minds, give us this day our daily bread, and forgive us our trespasses as we forgive those who trespassed against us. And lead us not into temptation but deliver us from evil, for Thine is the kingdom, and the power, and the glory, forever. Amen!

We were some praying people! Tears were falling, hugs were given, care packages were received, and farewells with best wishes for all mankind were taking place.

All the while, America and the rest of the world had fallen prey to a pandemic of fear and division. Eventually, things would slowly reopen because there was a new vaccine created to combat the virus. Some people were in favor of the shot while others didn't believe it had been tested long enough to be injected into their bodies.

The people who chose not to get vaccinated had to face adverse effects that came in the form of various mandates. Specifically, they were told not to return to work, school, or other normal daily activities until they did one of two things—one, tested negative for the covid virus with a test you could buy at any local pharmacy, or two, decided to receive the vaccine and get a covid card to prove it.

I even heard a well-known evangelist say in a news conference that if Jesus was walking the face of the earth in our day, He would also take the vaccine.

Blasphemy, to say the least! I couldn't believe my ears, and I couldn't believe what he said. These words rang aloud in my heart and mind, "Jesus said, 'I am the resurrection and the life. He that believeth in me, though he were dead, yet shall he live!'"

The church had now fallen in line with the government. The separation of church and state no longer held precedence. America had now fallen by the wayside. For a country whose motto was "In God We Trust," never once did we come together as a nation to call upon His Name and to ask for wisdom, knowledge, and understanding. We chose to leave the matter to the minds of the experts and professionals who had no idea how to handle it in the first place.

Meanwhile, the enemy was at work the whole time, using two of his tactics—fear and confusion—while bringing forth division in every sector of our daily lives. We were no longer a nation united but were instead a nation divided. We spent our days trying to adapt to what they called "the new normal". The effects of the mandates that the government imposed on the people shattered our ability to connect and reconnect with others, to build and rebuild relationships.

After continuous months of lockdown and finally being able to step outside and live again, many found themselves still dealing with the aftermath. The confusion and fear remained, being two extremely hard emotions to overcome because they manifest both mentally and physically and can only be overcome by assurance and peace. Yet, this peace is not just any old peace and definitely is not as the world brings peace. Rather, it is a true peace that surpasses all understanding, bringing in an assurance that only Jesus can provide.

As many grew lonely and bored, the need and want for human interaction and companionship became even more of a focal point. Yet, God was already hard at work, long before any of this had come to pass. He sent forth a ministry, not only given to me but to everyone all over this world, which is called the Ministry of Reconciliation. This ministry would bring all people together, being reconciled one to another—one person at a time, one relationship at a time, one prayer at a time—as all things are reconciled to Him, through Him, and for Him.

Although it's been four years now, many are still shaken by the fear that is still lingering. Many are scared by news coverage and reports of covid cases on the rise. Those who have lost loved ones to it now take no chances of catching it. The wounds are still fresh, and the hurt is real.

Removing the hurt and fear from people's hearts and minds is a long process. We, too, can help, as God has dealt every man a measure of faith. It's by faith we even have the capacity to believe. It's through faith, and faith alone, that we are able to stand in such daunting times.

"Faith is the substance of things hoped for, the evidence of things not seen. Through faith, we understand that the worlds were framed by the word of God, so that things which are seen were not made of things which do appear."

It's by these very words that we are able to overcome. We are able to move from fear to faith, becoming more than conquerors by Him who has created us.

The first step towards reconciliation is prayer, which consists of healing for yourself as well as for others. The next step is to allow the healing process to begin to take place in your hearts, minds, bodies, and souls. The final step is to live it out. Once again, you are being set free to open up your heart to so many others out there who once felt like you.

Please, trust me on this that there are others who love and need you. Your life and your story matters to those you know and even to those you don't. Opening up your heart is truly an act of love that not only changes you but also changes all those who surround you.

As I shared my story in part with all those I've encountered, family and friends included, everyone told me that I should write a book. I told them that I felt that I would one day, but it wouldn't happen until the Lord called me to do so when the time was right.

In my travels across America in working to bring forth the Ministry of Reconciliation, I came across a place where I had never been. I had only come across it online but immediately felt a deep connection to it and began researching it for several months. This place is called Lake Waccamaw, and it's located in North Carolina. So, I found an Airbnb and made a reservation for a month.

One week before I arrived, I started having flashbacks of my life. It was as if I was actually reliving each memory and able to see every little detail. I couldn't figure out why this was happening until, one night, I was reading the book of First Kings about a man named Josiah.

As I finished the chapter, the Lord spoke to me and told me, "You have a story of your own to write. It is time to share Our Story."

Once I arrived and got settled in, I began to write the book. While at times it has been hard and tears have streamed down my face, a healing was taking place that I, in fact, didn't realize I needed.

Writing this book has been nothing more than a true labor of love. Although this is only a small chapter in the greatest story ever written, I know that God is not only writing my greatest love story but yours as well.

As I concluded writing this book, the Lord provided a more detailed revelation of the vision of the two paths. I wish to share the deeper meaning with you here.

The dark, narrow, and windy road was the path I had to take to encounter all the people I've met. The path proved to be challenging, while the storms of life—even strong at times—came and went, allowing me to overcome many different obstacles and certain situations intended to stop me.

The two paths that came back to the same starting point were both narrow, being the only road that truly leads us back to Him. Although it may have many extensions to it, the path eventually becomes straight. "Broad is the way that leadeth to destruction, but narrow is the way which leadeth unto life, and there will be few that find it."

The color red of the church house is symbolic of the blood that Jesus shed on Calvary for you and me as He paid a debt for our sins that we could not. In fact, He gave Himself as a ransom for all mankind, covering us as a shelter from the storms.

All the people inside the red church are the people that God allowed me to impact—those from my group page, those whom I met on the streets and within my travels, and even those who may be reading this book now and in the future.

The silhouette of the woman holding her child inside the church is that some kind of wonderful woman I prayed for while being unaware that one like her even existed. We are happily married and share a beautiful newborn baby boy!

She and I share the same passion. She is kind, compassionate, caring, and full of grace and mercy—not only to our son and me but to many others that WE have encountered on a daily basis. But that's a story for another day!

The short walk to the rampart to see the grandeur of the mountains was another symbolic visual that my journey was now over, bringing into reality that there is no journey too great, or mountain too high, or valley too deep that the Love of God cannot reach.

The Cross is another significant sign to all men, women, and children. It tells us the story of a Man who, in one hand, held the hand of God and, in the other hand, held the hand of mankind, thus reconciling us back to Him through His death and blood on the Cross.

Jesus's Unfailing Love and Desire to connect His creation to the Creator gave us the Ministry of Reconciliation. "To wit, that God was in Christ, reconciling the world unto Himself, not imputing their trespasses unto them; and hath committed unto us the WORD of reconciliation."

He truly has done amazing things and will continue to do amazing things, as His Word will endure forever!

Matters of the Heart

A s I began to look back at my life and the legacy my parents left behind, I can remember a lesson my mother taught me when I was a young boy about the difference between a house and a home.

"A house is just a structure where people's belongings are kept. But a home is a place where memories are made, and love is found by all who dwell within it and amongst it."

My mother taught me that a home is where your heart is—a place that could travel with you wherever you went, keeping with you all the memories that you made wherever you were.

Memories that you both cherish and treasure are tucked safely away within the deep caverns of your heart. These stories, if you will, may be subconsciously kept for yourself or even shared with others any time you choose—just like the stories I have now shared with each and every one of you.

That lesson is what my mother meant by saying, "Look deep into your heart. You will see that I've always been there."

She not only wanted me to see all the memories we once shared, but she also wanted me to see all those who spoke over my life—in fact, praying over me. She and my father knew that I had a calling on my life that was much different than that of others.

I personally believe that she knew her time was short. Although she desired to see me walk in my calling, she knew that wasn't going to happen within the time she had left. So, she did the best thing that she could ever do for me by placing me in the hands of God.

My mother knew how God had always been gracious to her and my father and all those who they surrounded themselves with. She knew by placing me in the hands of God that He would not only continue to love me and protect me, but He would eventually reveal His plan for my life in His timing.

I think, in some ways, it broke her heart that she wouldn't be here to see it—to watch me become the man God intended me to be, and to watch as I would walk according to His plan and purpose for my life.

After all, as a child and a young man, I watched as my parents lived out their calling. It truly was a sight to see. My mother desired the very best for me in life, just like any good parent wants for all of their children.

She gave me that life verse, which says, "For where your treasure is, there will your heart be also."

She was sending me on a journey to seek this very thing out. She knew that whenever she threw something like that at me, and I didn't understand what she was saying, I would research it, stopping at nothing until I finally figured it out, no matter how long it would take. It was a message from the grave—the last mission she would ever ask of me again.

What I found out was that while I was going through all those trials and tribulations in my life—

the hurt, the pain, the grief, the depression, and the anguish—God had a replacement for each and every one of them. He has a treasure chest Full of Love, Full of Compassion, Full of Grace, and Full of Mercy—and anything else you might need. He desires to exchange all of our bad for His Good.

I discovered that my treasures were found with God and the hearts of men, women, and children, including those of you who have been hurt by life and its many tragedies that are unbeknown to us.

I now know that God Himself desires to turn our sorrow into joy. The depths of His Love for us are far greater than we will ever know. The measure by which He provides it—giving us strength, courage, hope, and faith—actually prepares us, as it makes us stronger spiritually, emotionally, physically, and mentally! He truly gives us the power from within to overcome and conquer all things, taking us from a place of fear and doubt to a place of faith and hope, having confidence in who He is.

After seeing the impact in my life of what my mother had done by placing me in the hands of God, I too have now placed all four of my children in His hands. I honestly feel that it's the greatest thing a parent can do for their children.

As a young child, I came across this verse that said, "Call unto me, and I will answer thee, and shew thee great and mighty things, which thou knowest not."

This verse drew my attention and curiosity. I never forgot it and always wondered what it truly meant. I never imagined that God has ways that are truly indescribable when teaching and revealing many different things to us. For instance, He reveals Himself through dreams and visions, a word of knowledge, and even personal encounters!

His ways are not at all our ways but are proof positive that He knows exactly what He's doing. He handles each of us in very different ways, as He continues to create us to be the masterpiece that He knew we would become and desired us to be. This doesn't just happen throughout birth—it happens throughout our entire lifetime.

It's the trials and tribulations that mold us into the very person we become. We choose to allow them to devour us, or we choose to overcome them. But, truly overcoming and conquering them requires help from the Lord. It requires us to come to a place in our life with need as we are finally ready to surrender—a need so great that man alone cannot provide all the help. The only choice we are left with is the right choice—to surrender and call upon His name.

As I've been traveling, I have met those who have been searching for answers and those who have been running from their calling. As I came across their paths, I spoke with these people, sharing with them things that spoke to their particular situations. I spoke from my heart as I, too, understood what they were going through.

They sat there in tears and looked at me in my eyes to say that they had been in prayer, that they had been seeking answers, and that no one could have known how to respond to such a situation unless God had revealed it to them.

Each person was left with only one possible answer, saying, "It was God who sent you to me."

Those who were running from their calling just automatically said to me, "I know why you're here. You've been sent to light a fire underneath me so that I, too, will answer the call."

At first, I didn't know how to take any of that. After all, I'm just a man like everyone else, but I realized that was God's way of confirming to me I was doing exactly what He called me to do, and that I was on the path He had specifically laid out just for me. It's amazing to know that He's watching over you and that He's truly directing your path.

As I continued to think back, recalling the prayer I made in asking Jesus to share His heart with me so that I could love others as He does, I didn't realize that He would also share His passion with me, which is a desire to dwell with and amongst His people. That, to me alone, is just mind-blowing in and of itself.

I learned that He desires to put broken people back together again, especially those who have a broken spirit—a broken and contrite heart, which is a feeling or action expressing remorse or repentance and affected by guilt and shame.

As God begins His work on us, He starts from the inside out—starting with our hearts by plucking out deeply seated roots that have now sprung up inside us with spiritually deadly effects. As He does this, it makes room for new growth. He plants seeds of righteousness within us, which will now grow from our hearts to our minds and flow throughout our bodies.

It doesn't stop there, as He continues to place us in the fire, refining us by drawing out our broken and sinful ways so we can stand pure and righteous before Him. It truly is an amazing process and only one that He can perform.

He then takes the man and blesses him with promise, telling us that He, Jesus, has set the matter of life and death before us. Blessings and curses, life and death. He tells us to choose life, not death; blessings, not curses. He then reveals His many blessings of life to us through His word by saying,

Blessed are the poor in spirit: for theirs is the kingdom of heaven.

Blessed are they that mourn: for they shall be comforted.

Blessed are the meek: for they shall inherit the earth.

Blessed are they which do hunger and thirst after righteousness: for they shall be filled.

Blessed are the merciful: for they shall obtain mercy.

Blessed are the pure in heart: for they shall see God.

Blessed are the peacemakers: for they shall be called the children of God.

Blessed are they which are persecuted for righteousness' sake: for theirs is the kingdom of heaven.

Blessed are ye, when men shall revile you, and persecute you, and shall say all manner of evil against you falsely, for my sake.

Rejoice, and be exceedingly glad: for great is your reward in heaven: for so persecuted the prophets which were before you.

Can you just imagine what my life would have looked like without God? My obituary would have read something like this—

Donald T. Hardison, II, suddenly and unexpectedly passed away from a drug overdose.

The Coroner's Verdict on the matter states, "Be it remembered that this information was given to me, that the dead body of Donald T. Hardison, II, has been found alone in his apartment, slumped over his coffee table. It is my opinion that Donald T. Hardison, II, died of a self-induced drug overdose."

Manner of Death: Self-ingested dose of a deadly poison (cocaine).

Ruling: Accidental suicide.

He leaves behind his loving children and will be missed by those who knew him. He was just twenty-eight years old. Yet another unnecessary and tragic loss of life in the war against drugs.

STOP, PAUSE, and THINK about this. There would be NO story, NO real legacy.

People would merely stop to say, "What a shame! His father first and now his son!" While pondering the thought, asking, "What will become of his children?"

OH!! I THANK GOD THAT'S NOT MY STORY!!! But if not for the Love of God, the Grace of God, the Mercy of God, and the Faithfulness of God to His very own words and promises, I would not be here today!

OH!! HOW I THANK GOD that He spared my life. I THANK HIM for the fact that He has never left me or forsaken me and that His love for me is unfailing!

I THANK HIM for allowing me to have an impact on the lives of so many others all across the world, knowing that what He has done for me, He desires to do for each and every one of you, if you just Dare to Believe!

In closing, allow me to share my final thoughts with you. That which is taking place in the "so-called church" or the "church of today" is not of God, nor will He and His Holy Spirit be present in such a place. He is not at all pleased as His Word is being blasphemed throughout all the land. He has told us through His Word that these things would happen, and that judgment is coming.

But, like any good Father, He seeks to protect His children and has instructed us to "come out from amongst them and be ye separate." He has asked us to learn from Him and His Holy Spirit Who is also the Comforter and Teacher Who will lead us into all Truth.

While my story has now been told, and my journey is now over, I know that my "Quest in Search of Truth" will never end. There is always a deeper truth to be found that brings forth a much greater wisdom which I desire to seek out, knowing that I'm not yet a perfect man but seek to become a better man today than I was yesterday, and having read a verse that says, "Mark the perfect man, for the end of that man is Peace!"

I am now forty-seven years old and honestly have no idea what my future holds. However, I know Who holds my future. I just know that God is not finished with me yet. As I have now been refined in the fire, I know that I am able to withstand any storm or any attack that may come my way. I am now able to stand in the valley of the shadow of death with God by my side and Boldly Declare: "Come What May, My God is Able!"

My greatest goal in life is one that I will never see here on earth but hope to obtain as I pass from this life into eternity, desiring to hear these words spoken by the King of Glory, saying, "Well Done Thou Good and Faithful Servant, Enter into Thy Rest!"

* * *

I would like to thank you from the bottom of my heart for allowing me to share my story with each and every one of you. Please know that my prayers are with you and for you.

Just like the ones whom you never met and did not know were praying for you, I know that this assurance will bring you peace to know that while you sleep and have not a clue, there are others who care enough about mankind—and you—to seek the face of God on your behalf!

We truly are set free by the blood of the Lamb and by the word of our testimony!

There is No Greater Love!

A Letter to My Children

I hope and pray these words find you well and that you may now see the legacy given to us by the greatest Power of all. With Him, we have the ability to overcome and conquer all things that stand in our way—even things sent to destroy us.

This message of truth is what your grandparents left us out of great love and respect, that our legacy will live on forever, not only for me but for all four of you, and even for your own children one day and the generations that follow. They also left us with the ability to truly Touch the lives of all those we know and don't know.

As your Father, I want you to know about the Heritage of our family, knowing you never really got the opportunity to know your grandmother or your great-grandmother. Just as she taught me to store these memories within my heart, I hope you will cherish them and do the same.

The same holds true for your grandfather and great-grandfather. Life isn't at all easy. Hardships will come, and they will go. It's what we choose to do and how we choose to react when the bottom in life falls out from underneath us that counts.

Always know that others are watching you, even if you don't see them. How we choose to endure these unexpected things will speak volumes to those who watch on.

Ask yourselves what message of love and hope you would like others to see in you, as we know, Love knows no bounds and will stop at nothing to be made whole again.

I am blessed beyond measure to finally have had the opportunity to share our Heritage, Legacy, and Truth with you. Even as hard as it may have been to hear some of these things, I know it will only be a great benefit to you now and in the future.

It has been my greatest honor to have learned what is truly meant by these words, knowing, "Greater love hath no man than this, that a man lay down his life for his friends," while being able to show you, as I have lived this out both day and night. Now having answered some of the questions you may have had about your family who loves and cherishes you so very much!

I Love you Always and Forever,

Your Dad

Please Leave a Review

First and foremost, thank you for joining me on my journey! If you enjoyed reading my memoir, please be kind and leave a review on the site where you purchased the book. Reviews greatly help both authors and readers find the best books, so I look forward to hearing how my story influenced you.

Also by the Author

My multi-award-winning memoir, *A Break in the Silence: Reconciled or Forgotten?*

Scan the QR code to purchase on Amazon:

About the Author

 The author is a man who has sought to live above the norm of what society deems responsible living. He has a passion and a drive to reach the lives and hearts of others. He desires to share his passion with you. While many don't understand it, his mission is to help bring you understanding throughout his book. To contact the author, you may visit his website or email him at the following:
https://www.thequestinsearchoftruth.com
thequestinsearchoftruth1@gmail.com.